Knowing
& Loving
the Bible

KNOWING
&LOVING
THE BIBLE

CATHERINE MARTIN

HARVEST HOUSE PUBLISHERS

EUGENE, OREGON

KNOWING AND LOVING THE BIBLE
Copyright © 2007 by Catherine Martin
Published by Harvest House Publishers
Eugene, Oregon 97402

Library of Congress Cataloging-in-Publication Data
Martin, Catherine, 1956-
  Knowing and loving the Bible / Catherine Martin.
    p. cm.
  Includes bibliographical references.
  ISBN-13: 978-0-7369-1894-7 (pbk.)
  ISBN-10: 0-7369-1894-9 (pbk.)
  1. Bible—Study and teaching. 2. Bible—Criticism, interpretation, etc. I. Title.
BS600.3.M32 2007
220.071—dc22
                                                              2006021726

07 08 09 10 11 12 13 14 15 / VP-SK / 10 9 8 7 6 5 4 3 2 1

Dedicated to Josh McDowell,
who taught me the significance of the
authority of God and His Word,
who has been my great example
as a servant in ministry,
and who has helped me understand
what it means to love the Lord.
May his tribe increase.

If anyone really loves me, he will observe my teaching, and my Father will love him, and both of us will come in face-to-face fellowship with him; yes, we will make our special dwelling place with him.

JOHN 14:23
WILLIAMS NEW TESTAMENT

Nothing is perfect except your words. Oh, how I love them. I think about them all day long.

PSALM 119:96-97 TLB

CONTENTS

FOREWORD

When I set out to refute Christianity, I sought to discredit the reliability of the Bible. If I could demonstrate that the Bible was not historically reliable, I could disprove the claims of Christ. My idea backfired because the evidences of the reliability of Scripture were overwhelming. I became convinced of the truth of the Bible, God's love for me, and His desire for a relationship with me. The Bible is not just instructions or guidelines—it is how God has chosen to reveal Himself to you and me. When you hold the Bible in your hands, you are holding more than a book; its words will show you the God who gives you life, meaning, and purpose.

If such benefits are waiting for us in the Bible, it stands to reason that we need to get into the Bible for ourselves. The Bible is a book to study and understand—a place where you feel at home. The Bible, God's love letter to the world, is a treasure waiting to be discovered. How can such a discovery occur? Catherine Martin's *Knowing and Loving the Bible* will help you open the pages of the Bible, day by day, and discover its riches. Ultimately, after your time in this 30-day journey, you will love God more and wholeheartedly serve Him.

Dottie and I have known Catherine for more than 25 years and have served together with her on the Campus Crusade for Christ staff. She is one of the most joy-filled, Spirit-controlled, energetic, and enthusiastic servants of God I know. People used to call our office just to hear her friendly voice on the telephone! We have watched the Lord open exciting doors for her with Quiet Time Ministries and the books she has written.

If you spend just 30 days in *Knowing and Loving the Bible,* your life will be affected. Before long, you will be opening the pages of your own Bible to discover what God has to say to you. When you do, you will experience the great reward that comes to all those who have given time and energy to the study of the Bible—God will reveal Himself to you. And when He does, you will know what others down through the centuries who have cherished their Bibles have known—an intimate, life-giving, dynamic relationship with the Lord Jesus Christ.

Josh McDowell

Face to Face

ANNIE JOHNSON FLINT

Over there 'twill all be clear, though I see but dimly here,
For—what glory when I see Him face to face!
Face to face—and that forever;
Face to face, where naught can sever;
I shall see Him in His beauty, face to face;
I have caught faint glimpses here,
Seen through many a falling tear,
But—what glory when I see Him face to face!

INTRODUCTION

While I was browsing through a furniture store, my eyes were drawn to an old, tattered Bible, a mere prop on one of the bookshelves. I immediately pulled it from the shelf, opened it, and began flipping through the worn pages. To my surprise and delight, I saw that every page had scribbled notations, underlined words, and countless penned comments in the margins. Once I had convinced the salesman to let me buy it, I hurried home with my treasure. Time stood still for me as I sat quietly, scanning the comments and absorbing the notations, all the while trying to read between the lines. Who was this person? What kind of life did she lead? When I had read to my heart's content, I searched the front pages of the Bible. Oddly, the owner's name was nowhere to be found. Fitting, perhaps. I had been given an intimate glimpse into the heart of an anonymous saint who had experienced a rich devotional life with God in His Word. Whoever had owned that Bible had spent much time with God there. She had wrestled with the words, rejoiced with the words, and treasured the words. As I closed the

Bible, I knew one thing was certain—that beloved saint knew and loved the Bible, and as a result, she knew and loved God.

When I first opened my own Bible as a new Christian, I felt like a traveler in a foreign land. I had absolutely no idea where to begin, but I knew the Bible somehow held the key to my relationship with God. I decided to explore various chapters of the Bible that interested me—first the Psalms and then John, Genesis, Romans, and even Revelation. Soon, certain verses and phrases in the Bible became familiar to me. As I read further, I was amazed to discover that God was speaking to me personally. Each verse seemed significant to my life. I began underlining verses and writing some thoughts and personal responses in the margins of my Bible. As a result, by reading the Bible, I was growing closer to God with each passing day. God became my first true love, and He impressed on my heart, in a deep and lasting way, that I must sacrifice time and energy to live in His Word, to know it, to understand it, and to love it. Many quiet times with the Lord later, I can truly say that my intentional response was well worth the effort. The Bible was the key that unlocked the door to the great adventure of knowing God, to an exciting romance. And 30 years later, this romance with the Word of God still holds that excitement for me. When I open the Word and begin reading, I see His words come alive. I find my life changed. I find myself drawing closer to God and experiencing His presence. My romance with the Word gives me what I want more than anything else: intimacy with God.

If you had the opportunity to take the 30-day journey of *Six Secrets to a Powerful Quiet Time* (Harvest House Publishers, 2006), you discovered the joy of radical intimacy with God through quiet time with Him. You learned the P.R.A.Y.E.R. Quiet Time Plan: Prepare Your Heart, Read and Study God's Word, Adore God in Prayer, Yield Yourself to God, Enjoy His Presence, and Rest in His Love. And you were encouraged to use a journal or the *Quiet Time Notebook* in your quiet time to help you on your journey to intimacy with God.

I want to invite you to a new, life-changing, 30-day journey to fall in love, face-to-face with God in His Word, the Bible. Whether you are new to the Bible or have lived in it for 50 years, this journey will revive your heart, renew your spirit, and refresh your soul. In *Knowing and Loving the Bible* we continue the journey of intimacy with God by answering the question, how can I come face-to-face with God in the Bible? This 30-day journey is a romance—the great romance—between you and God in His Word. How can the words in the Bible leap off the pages and move in your heart? How is this romance possible? The psalmist says, "Friendship with God is reserved for those who reverence Him. With them alone He shares the secrets of His promises" (Psalm 25:14 TLB). Where can you discover the great romance of knowing God—His heart, His ways, His character, His personality, His feelings, His desires? In the Bible. Peter says that the promises of God found in the Word of God are "your tickets to participation in the life of God" (2 Peter 1:4 MSG). Where can you fall in love with Jesus? In the Bible. There you will find Jesus, who is "the radiance of His glory and the exact representation of His nature" (Hebrews 1:3). Where can you find the romance of life itself? In the Bible. The psalmist says, "Turn my eyes from worthless things; and give me life through your word" (Psalm 119:37 NLT). The Bible, the Word of God, is where you meet and fall in love with God. This 30-day journey is written with one great purpose in mind: that you will never let your Bible sit on a shelf but that you will live in its pages and let its words live in your heart.

Knowing and Loving the Bible is my response to what I believe is the greatest crisis in the church today: an undermining of the authority of the Word of God. Statistics demonstrate that of those who attend church, only 45 percent ever open their Bibles outside of their time in church. Many in the church no longer look to the Bible as the handbook for life or let it guide their attitudes, beliefs, and actions. Instead, many people substitute man's words, thoughts, and feelings for God's words, thoughts, and feelings. I believe we need a revival that takes us back to the Bible, a revival that raises up people who are more concerned with what God says than what man says. In this revival, people will take closed Bibles off the bookshelves and open them, study them, trust them, pray over them, believe them, and apply them to their lives. I believe God is looking for men and women who will step out from the crowd, grab the Bible, know it, love it, and give it away. I believe God is looking for those who, like Moses, will turn aside to listen when God speaks. And that is what happens in the Bible: God speaks. In

Knowing and Loving the Bible you will discover the significance of the Bible, where the Bible came from, many ways to devotionally study the Bible in your quiet time, and practical ideas to help develop a rich love for God's Word. This book is not meant to be an exhaustive treatise on how to study the Bible. Instead, it is designed to encourage you to know and love the Bible and use it in your daily quiet time with the Lord. My prayer is that as a result of your 30-day journey through *Knowing and Loving the Bible,* you will love and cherish the Bible as a gift and treasure from God Himself.

HOW TO USE *KNOWING AND LOVING THE BIBLE*

Each week you will *read, respond,* and *experience:*

Read. In each day's reading, interact with the ideas by underlining what is significant to you and writing your comments in the margins. This book will encourage you to learn, grow, and develop a great love for the Word of God. Please mark it up and make it yours!

Respond. To help you think through and apply all that is written here, I have included a devotional response section at the end of each day. You'll find a key verse for you to meditate on and memorize. For further thought, I have provided questions for you to consider. Finally, you'll find a place for you to express your thoughts and respond to what you have read. This is your opportunity to dialogue with God about knowing and loving the Bible and drawing near to Him.

Experience. For practical application, each week ends with a complete, interactive quiet time that emphasizes the principles you will have learned in that section. Use the blank Notes page to record what you learn from the companion DVD to *Knowing and Loving the Bible.*

In addition, you can *share your journey.* Read what others are learning on their journey through *Knowing and Loving the Bible* and share your own insights with others throughout the world, posting your thoughts on the Quiet Time Ministries discussion board at www.quiettimecafe.com.

SUGGESTED APPROACHES FOR *KNOWING AND LOVING THE BIBLE*

You can benefit from this book in several ways:

- *Sequentially.* You may want to read the book a day at a time and implement the principles before moving to the next chapter.

- *Topically.* You may have specific topics of interest to you. If that is the case, you can look at the table of contents and focus on those topics.

- *Devotionally.* You may choose to read this book over 30 days. The days are divided into five sections so that you can take five weeks to read and think about knowing and loving the Bible. It can be a 30-day adventure!

SUGGESTED SETTINGS FOR *KNOWING AND LOVING THE BIBLE*

Personal and private. This is the kind of book you can read again and again. It will encourage you to draw near to God, especially if you are in a season where you have lost a habit of time with your Lord in His Word or you need to shake up your quiet time because it has become lackluster and routine. You might even want to take this book and spend some extended time in a beautiful setting to revive and refresh your relationship with the Lord. It's a retreat in a book!

Small groups. I encourage you to travel on this 30-day journey with some friends. What a joy it is to share what you are learning with others who also love the Lord. You can use the questions at the end of each day for your discussion together. Appendix 1 contains additional discussion questions. This book is perfect for Sunday school classes, Bible study groups, church congregations, or your family devotions.

Ministry revival campaign. You may also desire to use this book as a 30-day intensive campaign to teach, revive, and inspire those in your ministry. A campaign like this will help grow your ministry as new small groups are formed. Included in appendix 1 are weekly discussion questions for small groups. Six accompanying messages on DVD are available from Quiet Time Ministries, covering the introductory week through week five. For more information on using this book as a spiritual growth campaign for your group, go to www.lovingthebible.com or www.quiettime.org.

Enough preparation: let's begin the journey! *Knowing and Loving the Bible* is my conversation with you about God and His Word. I invite you to engage in this great romance with God and His Word. It is not simply a romance with words in a book, but a romance with a Person, Jesus Christ, the King of kings and Lord of lords, through the Bible. I would not have you stand on the sidelines watching someone else enjoy this divine romance—I would rather you experience for yourself the touch of His love, the healing warmth of His comfort, and the joy of His Spirit. May God richly bless you on this journey.

THE DIVINE
ROMANCE

Days 1-6

THE INVITATION TO THE DIVINE ROMANCE

Draw near to God and He will draw near to you.

JAMES 4:8

God wants a face-to-face relationship with you, a divine romance that He initiates. You respond to His overtures of love by drawing near and pursuing Him. James says, "Draw near to God and He will draw near to you" (James 4:8). How can you draw near? By studying, line by line, His love letter to you—the Bible—that you may know, understand, and love Him. When you open the pages of the Bible, His written words to you, and begin to read what He has to say, you are engaging in the divine romance, responding to the God who loves you. Knowing and loving the Bible are as essential to spiritual life as breathing is to physical life. A.W. Tozer, in *The Pursuit of God,* encourages us to develop the lifelong habit of spiritual response. Knowing and loving the Bible is your spiritual response to the divine initiative of God. It includes taking interludes alone with God in the Bible—respites with Him that refresh your heart and nurture your spirit. To know and love the Bible means to live in God's Word in such a way that God's Word lives in you.

Early in my relationship with God, I opened the Bible to Jeremiah 31:3 and read, "I have loved you with an everlasting love." Those words were spoken to the people of Israel, but they also define the boundaries and quality of God's love for me. He loves me always and forever. Those words struck at the core of my being and caused my heart to burn with a passion for the God who loved me with an everlasting love. The romance between God and mankind is far more exciting and mysterious than that of a Shakespearean drama. Sentimentalism is replaced with agape love. Sensualism is replaced with commitment. Mysticism is replaced with communion. God's divine romance is practical; it's essential to a rich and meaningful everyday life.

Face-to-face fellowship is God's idea, created by His initiative, and fulfilled by His design. The Bible tells us that "the LORD used to speak to Moses face-to-face, just as a man speaks to his friend" (Exodus 33:11). In fact, God told Moses that He was passionate about His relationship with him (Exodus 33:12). Jesus says, "If anyone really loves me, he will observe my teaching, and my Father will love him, and both of us will come in face-to-face fellowship with him; yes, we will make our special dwelling place with him" (John 14:23 Williams New Testament). The Lord wants to meet with you in face-to-face fellowship as He lives with you and in you.

Throughout the Bible we see God's desire for fellowship. God walked with Adam and Eve in the garden of Eden (Genesis 3:8). He dwelt in the tabernacle at the time of the Exodus (Exodus 29:43-46) and in the temple at the time of Solomon (2 Chronicles 7:1-3). He *tabernacled* (lived) among His people in the Person of Jesus according to John 1:14 and now makes His home in the hearts of His people through the indwelling Holy Spirit (John 14:15-23). The ultimate fulfillment of God's desire will be seen as the holy city, new Jerusalem, comes down out of heaven (Revelation 21:2-4). God's desire is clear. He wants to fellowship with you. How can such a fellowship occur?

Face-to-face with God means heart-to-heart with God—God

speaking from His heart straight to your heart—an intimate romance joining your heart to the heart of God. It is a radical intimacy with the God who created you, loves you, and wants you for all eternity. How does God communicate with you so that you may hear Him speak? God's Word is filled with His words. If you want to know what God has to say to you and fellowship with the One who loves you more than life itself (John 15:13), open the pages of your Bible.

God speaks to us in the Bible. Behind the written Word is the very voice of God Himself. The three Greek nouns for *word* in the New Testament reveal that God speaks (*lalia*), He has something to say (*rhema*), and He says it in a language we can understand (*logos*). Jesus uses all three of these Greek words when He talks with the religious leaders of the day about hearing His Word (John 8:42-47). The important point in the use of these three Greek words is that behind the written Word is the Person of God Himself, speaking to you from all of Scripture. God wants you to know you are never alone when you are reading or studying His Word; He wants you to be assured of His ongoing presence with you. The One who said to Joshua, "Just as I was with Moses, so I will be with you" (Joshua 1:5 ESV) is also the One who says to you, "I will never leave you nor forsake you" (Hebrews 13:5 ESV). He is not only with you but also has something to say to you.

A.W. Tozer, in *The Pursuit of God*, contends that God, by His nature, is continuously articulate, filling the world with His speaking voice. "God's word in the Bible can have power only because it corresponds to God's word in the universe. It is the present Voice which makes the written Word all-powerful. Otherwise it would lie locked in slumber within the covers of a book."[1] When you open the Bible and begin to read, God is there with you, speaking to your heart. You might be reading Psalms, Proverbs, the Gospels, or Revelation. Regardless of where you are in the Bible, God is there, waiting for you to turn to Him, meet with Him, hear what He has to say to you, and respond to what He has said.

WHY KNOW AND LOVE THE BIBLE?

When you open the pages of the Bible, what is going to help you know it and love it in such a way that you can hear what God has to say? The following truths about the Bible can motivate you as you spend time in God's Word:

- *The Bible is alive for you.* Hebrews 4:12 (NIV) says, "The word of God is living and active. Sharper than any double-edged sword, it penetrates even to dividing soul and spirit, joints and marrow; it judges the thoughts and attitudes of the heart." When you open the pages of the Bible, ask, *Lord, what do You want to say to me today?*

- *The Bible has a purpose for you.* In Isaiah 55:11 God says this about His Word, the Bible: "It will not return to Me empty, without accomplishing what I desire, and without succeeding in the matter for which I sent it." When you open the pages of the Bible, ask, *Lord, what do You want to do in and through me?*

- *The Bible changes your life.* Paul told Timothy, "All Scripture is inspired by God and is useful to teach us what is true and to make us realize what is wrong in our lives. It straightens us out and teaches us to do what is right" (2 Timothy 3:16 NLT). When you open the pages of the Bible, ask, *Lord, what areas of my life need transformation by You?*

A COMMITMENT TO KNOWING AND LOVING THE BIBLE

Billy Graham was asked what he would do if he knew he had only three years to live. He said he would spend two years studying the Word and one year preaching the gospel. Elmer Lappen, the director of Campus Crusade for Christ at Arizona State University, told me years ago that if he could live his life over, he would spend more time studying God's Word. Those two men have probably known and loved the Bible better than anyone I know. And yet they felt that they needed more time with God in His Word. As you embark on this 30-day journey, will you resolve to engage in this divine romance with God, step away from the crowd, and draw near to God in His Word, the Bible? If so, you are in for the time of your life—the great adventure of knowing God.

Billy Sunday captured the essence of the divine romance of God in His Word with these notes he kept in his Bible:

Twenty-nine years ago, with the Holy Spirit as my Guide, I entered at the portico of Genesis, walked down the corridor of the Old Testament art galleries, where pictures of Noah, Abraham, Moses, Joseph, Isaac, Jacob, and Daniel hung on the wall. I passed into the music room of the Psalms where the Spirit sweeps the keyboard of nature until it seems that every reed and pipe in God's great organ responds to the harp of David, the sweet singer of Israel. I entered the chamber of Ecclesiastes, where the voice of the preacher is heard, and into the conservatory of Sharon and the lily of the valley where sweet spices filled and perfumed my life. I entered the business office of Proverbs and on into the observatory of the prophets where I saw telescopes of various sizes pointing to far off events, concentrating on the bright and morning Star which was to rise above the moonlit hills of Judea for our salvation and redemption. I entered the audience room of the King of Kings, catching a vision written by Matthew, Mark, Luke, and John. Thence into the correspondence room with Paul, Peter, James, and John writing their Epistles. I stepped into the throne room of Revelation where tower the glittering peaks, where sits the King of Kings upon His throne of glory with the healing of nations in His hand, and I cried out: All hail the power of Jesus' name! Let angels prostrate fall; Bring forth the royal diadem and crown Him Lord of all.

My Response

DATE:

KEY VERSE: "Draw near to God and He will draw near to you" (James 4:8).

FOR FURTHER THOUGHT: Will you make the decision to pay the price in time and energy to know and love the Bible so that you may come face-to-face with God in His Word? Ask God now to prepare your heart as you begin this 30-day journey of knowing and loving the Bible. Write a letter to the Lord as a prayer to Him in the space provided.

MY RESPONSE: A Letter to the Lord

THE STORY OF
YOUR LIFE

*You will make known to me the path of
life; in Your presence is fullness of joy; in
your right hand there are pleasures forever.*

PSALM 16:11

God wants to tell a story to the world through you. It is a story of
your relationship with God as He speaks with you in the Bible.
God writes the story on your heart first, fashioning and transforming
you, making you His man or woman. Your story will unfold through
your fellowship with God as you meet with Him in His Word,
commune with Him, wrestle at times with Him, and ultimately yield
to His unrelenting love. You will be on a quest; it's what Tozer called
the pursuit of God. The psalmist said, "You will make known to me
the path of life; in your presence is fullness of joy; in your right hand
there are pleasures forever" (Psalm 16:11). And then the psalmist says in
Psalm 119:105, "Your Word is a lamp to my feet and a light to my path."
Every life tells a story. Consider any of the men or women in the Bible:
David, Moses, Abraham, Hannah, Paul. Each has a unique story God

tells through his or her life. And so it is with you. You will experience your meaning and purpose in life as you select a Bible, personalize it, live in it, understand what it says, and watch as God uses it to transform your life, reveal Himself to you, and unfold the story of your life.

My love for the Word of God began with *Marian's Book of Bible Stories*. My mother gave it to me when I was four years old. At first, she read it to me, story by story, and I hung on every word. I could not wait to hear what would happen with Moses as he crossed the Red Sea, David as he killed Goliath, or Jesus as He healed the blind man. These were not stories to me; they were reality. God was real. Using the stories as examples, I began talking with God about everything in my life just as Moses, David, and Jesus had done in the stories. Later, when the words became easier for me to read as a little girl, I sat for hours with that Bible storybook and read those stories over and over again, the vivid pictures of the historical events becoming etched in my mind.

My mother gave me a white zippered King James Version Bible when I was ten, but I did not seem to understand it until five years later when I invited Jesus Christ as Savior into my life. Suddenly, the words came alive, especially the New Testament stories about the life of Jesus, Paul, and the disciples. I began highlighting my favorite verses with colored pencils.

Five years later I made the important decision to dedicate my whole life to the Lord. It was a day of surrender—a defining moment. I remember asking my roommate about types of Bibles because I wanted to commemorate this new direction in my life with a new Bible. My roommate recommended going to the Bible bookstore and getting a new translation—the New American Standard Bible. When I began reading the NASB, I found the verses opening up to me as a series of buried treasures, uncovered one by one, surprise after surprise. Soon I began to write the dates next to specific verses that influenced my life.

The next important step in my romance with God in His Word was my time with Thea Dryfhout, an older family friend who loved Jesus. Thea invited me to her house for a personal Bible study in Romans. (We never did get past Romans.) Thea read a few verses of Scripture and then read from Matthew Henry's commentary. Then she explained it all to me in her own words and answered my questions. This was an incredible time for me as I discovered powerful truths related to God and His ways. Thea knew God, and she knew His Word. When she prayed, she seemed to be looking directly at God. I wanted that kind of experience with God. You should have seen her Bible, the cover distressed, the pages worn, and oh, the vast underlining and notes. I wanted my Bible to look like that.

During my college years, I became involved with Campus Crusade for Christ, where I learned to put God's Word into action. I always had a choice: Did I believe God's Word, or did I believe my feelings and circumstances? I learned that I must have an objective faith in God's Word. I carried my Bible with me everywhere, even to a Campus Crusade summer project in Hawaii, selling pineapples to tourists and showing them Scripture at every opportunity.

Following college I served the Lord with the Josh McDowell Ministry in Campus Crusade for Christ. Through Josh, I learned about the authority of God and His Word; that God, through the Bible, possesses the supreme right to command my beliefs and actions. I made the decision to give more time and energy to reading and studying the Bible.

Soon after I was married, my romance with God's Word led me to Bible Study Fellowship and Precept Ministry International's Bible studies. From these studies I learned how to plumb the depths of Scripture, dig deeper, and rightly divide the truth of God's Word. At this time I began building a library of Bible study tools, spending hours scouring the shelves at Evangelical Bible Bookstore in San Diego. I often sat cross-legged on the floor in the Bible study tools section, surrounded myself with books, and studied how to use them. I gave lists of books I wanted most to my friends. Before long, I built a great library of Bible study tools that I use every day in my quiet time as I study God's Word.

At Bethel Theological Seminary, I had the great privilege to sit under professors such as Walter Wessel and Ronald Youngblood, translators of the New International Version. They opened up the world of biblical studies and interpretation, textual criticism, exegesis, and Greek and Hebrew translation. My love for God's Word deepened, and I began to regard God's Word with a serious passion that led to the founding of Quiet Time Ministries.

The result of this love affair with God in His Word has been a day-by-day adventure as God has met me in the deepest darkness and the grandest mountaintops. It has resulted in a story God is telling as He leads me on the path He has for me in life. He has given me the opportunity to watch Him work in the lives of others as I engage in the great adventure of knowing Him. And the story continues, even today, as I open the pages of His Word and draw near in face-to-face fellowship with Him.

THE STORIES GOD HAS TOLD

I derive great inspiration from the stories God has told through the lives of others. Those stories are filled with tears and triumph. Each person found his or her path in life by knowing God in His Word. I think of such great men and women of God as Oswald Chambers, Andrew Murray, A.W. Tozer, G. Campbell Morgan, John Henry Jowett, Octavius Winslow, Amy Carmichael, Hannah Whitall Smith, Darlene Diebler Rose, and Elisabeth Elliot. I am constantly reading about the lives of men and women who had hearts that beat for God and whose lives have impacted the world.

DISCOVERING YOUR SPIRITUAL STORY

And now, what about you? What is the story God is telling through you? Have you discovered His path for you? As you begin this 30-day journey, how would you describe your adventure in the Bible up to this point in your life? A casual acquaintance? A brief affair, now past? A sporadic friendship? Or a deep, abiding romance? Has your Bible been sitting on the shelf, or is it worn like Thea Dryfhout's? Regardless of where you are, you can know that the Lord desires this unique, intimate fellowship with you in His Word. And He wants to write His story in and through your life.

Your story begins with God. He is the one who dreamed of you and made you exactly the way you are with your gifts and talents. He has a plan and a purpose for you. Ephesians 2:10 tells us that "we are His workmanship, created in Christ Jesus for good works, which God prepared beforehand so that we would walk in them." The great drama, the great adventure, really occurs when you come to know Jesus and begin meeting with Him in His Word. Then God does great and mighty things in and through you, moment by moment and day by day.

The question is, how can you discover your spiritual story? How can you actually know and understand what God is doing? The secret is to look for it. God said in Jeremiah 29:13, "You will seek Me and find Me when you search for Me with all your heart." Your story really begins when you come to know God personally by establishing a relationship with Him. It includes receiving Jesus into your heart and life and, as a result, experiencing His forgiveness of your sins and eternal life. With hands extended He is inviting you to a relationship with Himself. A gift with all of its benefits doesn't become yours until you receive it. John tells us that "as many as received Him, to them He gave the right to become children of God, even to those who believe in His name" (John 1:12). If you have never established a relationship with God, you can start by praying a simple prayer like this: *Lord Jesus, I need You. Thank You for dying on the cross for my sins. I invite You into my life and ask You to forgive my sins and make me the person You want me to be. Amen.*

Once your relationship with God is established, the real story of your life begins as you get to know God and His ways. God writes your story, and your life speaks of His greatness and power. Moses asked God, "Let me know Your ways that I may know You, so that I may find favor in Your sight" (Exodus 33:13). Moses wanted to know God's ways. He wanted to know what God was doing. In this way, Moses could understand how God was working in his life and in the lives of the people of Israel. God often instructed Moses to write about events to create "a memorial" to His character and His ways (Exodus 17:14-15). Throughout the Old Testament, the Lord often directed His people to write and remember, to set up visual reminders of His awesome acts, and ultimately, to make memorials to Him all along the journey of life.

MAKE A MEMORIAL TO THE LORD

Following that Old Testament example and making memorials to the Lord has helped me see what God is doing in my own life. Making a memorial to the Lord can include setting aside time to review a year in your life and write down what God has done. You pay special attention to God and His ways and notice what He is doing in your life. You look ahead to the story of your life in the new year and plan spiritual goals. I like to set aside a morning or afternoon at the beginning of each new year to make a memorial to the Lord. I review the year and think about significant verses in the Bible, books I've read, spiritual lessons I've learned, things I've seen about God and His ways, and important events.

After my review, I like to think about the new year and look for God at work in my life by asking God to give me a word and a verse for the year. I like to write my word and verse on a bookmark to place in my Bible. I remember the year that Proverbs 3:5 was significant to me: "Trust in the LORD with all your heart, and do not lean on your own understanding." That year my word was *trust*. That was the year my mother experienced a terrible accident, and I spent weeks at the hospital with her during her recovery. I learned a lot about trust. I learned that trust is Total Reliance Under Stress and Trial.

Another year, during an illness with my husband, I noticed Luke 1:37 (NIV): "Nothing is impossible with God." One year I focused on the first four words of Genesis 8: "But God remembered Noah." And finally, Lamentations 3:21-24 became my verses for a year: "This I recall to my mind, therefore I have hope. The LORD's lovingkindnesses indeed never cease, for His compassions never fail. They are new every morning; great is Your faithfulness. 'The LORD is my portion,' says my soul, 'therefore I have hope in Him.'" That year my word was *hope*. And so all year long I looked for verses in the Bible that taught me about hope. And I learned that hope is Holding On with Patient Expectation.

I encourage you to take some time to make a memorial to the Lord and then ask Him to give you a word and a verse for the year. You will find a worksheet in appendix 2 to help you think and pray about these things. If you will take time to make a memorial to the Lord, God and His Word will become greater priorities in your life. And those priorities will help you decide day by day to spend quiet time with God and open the pages of the Bible to discover what God has to say to you.

Carl Lundquist, former president of Bethel College and Seminary, gives this explanation:

> Recollection consists of taking time to think gratefully about God's acts in our personal experience, or about His character as He has revealed it to us. Oftentimes we will be led to

recite to Him our experiences of His grace and to voice our gratitude to Him. The Psalmist did this often. Not only is the Psalter the prayer book of Israel in terms of confession and petition, but also in terms of its sheer contemplation of God and His works. There are many extended passages in which the Psalmist simply exults in what God has done in national history or in personal experience. He not only says thank you for immediate benefits, but he goes back over decades and centuries to detail what God has done and to praise Him for it.

May you fellowship with God in His Word and have an ocean of praise to Him for the story He is telling to the world through you.

My Response

DATE:

KEY VERSE: "You will make known to me the path of life; in Your presence is fullness of joy; in your right hand there are pleasures forever" (Psalm 16:11).

FOR FURTHER THOUGHT: What has been your adventure with God and His Word? Take a few moments now to recall the most important times of growth in your experience with God and His Word. You might think of these times as defining moments in your relationship with the Lord. Record these defining moments. Then schedule a time to make a memorial to the Lord and ask God to give you a word and verse for the year (see appendix 2).

MY RESPONSE:

WHY I LOVE
THE BIBLE

*Nothing is perfect except your
words. Oh, how I love them. I
think about them all day long.*

PSALM 119:96-97 TLB

Your relationship with God grows in proportion with your love for His Word, the Bible. The psalmist, in his conversation with the God he was growing to love, said, "Nothing is perfect except your words. Oh, how I love them. I think about them all day long" (Psalm 119:96-97). As you engage in this 30-day journey of knowing and loving the Bible, ask yourself, how much do I love the Bible? Do I love the Bible enough to open it daily and see God face to face?

I love the Bible because it encourages me. One morning I was feeling especially alone as I began my quiet time with the Lord. I wrote in my journal, "Lord, I need Your encouragement in my life today." I turned to *Morning and Evening* by Charles Spurgeon, and the reading for that day included the verse, "I will never leave you nor forsake you" (Joshua 1:5 NIV). Then I opened *My Utmost for His Highest* by Oswald

Chambers, and much to my surprise, he quoted the very same verse. Later, when I arrived at my office, I opened a card from a friend that quoted the same reassuring verse. Tears filled my eyes as I realized that the Lord was specifically encouraging me that day and letting me know He was with me, and I was not alone.

I love the Bible because it comforts me. "This is my comfort in my affliction, that Your Word has revived me" (Psalm 119:50). I have faced trials so difficult that I have been tempted to give up in despair. I turn to the words in the Bible in the hope that somewhere, somehow, God will give me comfort. And I am never disappointed. My Bible is underlined throughout, and the verses with the most marks are those where God gave me great comfort. I love Psalm 46:1, "God is our refuge and strength, a very present help in trouble." And Isaiah 41:10 has been very important to me: "Do not fear, for I am with you; do not anxiously look about you, for I am your God. I will strengthen you, surely I will help you, surely I will uphold you with My righteous right hand." And finally, Romans 8:37-39: "But in all these things we overwhelmingly conquer through Him who loved us. For I am convinced that neither death, nor life, nor angels, nor principalities, nor things present, nor things to come, nor powers, nor height, nor depth, nor any other created thing, will be able to separate us from the love of God, which is in Christ Jesus our Lord."

I love the Bible because it never changes. Jesus concluded the Sermon on the Mount with this illustration: "Therefore, everyone who hears these words of Mine and acts on them, may be compared to a wise man who built his house on the rock. And the rain fell, and the floods came, and the winds blew and slammed against that house; and yet it did not fall, for it had been founded on the rock" (Matthew 7:24-25). Oswald Chambers comments on this parable that "every spiritual castle will be tested by a three-fold storm—rain, floods and winds: the world, the flesh and the devil, and it will only stand if it is founded on the sayings of Jesus."[1] I choose to build my life on the Word of God.

I love the Bible because it is the authority for my belief. It possesses the supreme right to command my beliefs and my actions. When I was in seminary, a fellow student challenged one of my papers for a systematic theology class. He said to me "I have a real problem with what you said about election and God's choice of people." I said, "Oh, really? Well, which part did you not like?" He said, "All of it." And then he proceeded to rip apart my paper, point by point. On every point, I answered, "Well, God's Word says…" But he would disregard my response and move on to the next point. This happened again and again until suddenly a light went on in my head. I realized why we were having such a discrepancy in our beliefs. I asked, "Wait a minute. Tell me, what is the authority for your belief?" He responded, "The authority for my belief is the Word of God…and what I can comprehend with my rational mind." I said, "That's the difference between you and me. And we will never agree as long as that is your basis of authority. The authority for my belief is God's Word, the Bible. Period."

I love the Bible because it reveals Jesus. Jesus challenged the religious leaders of the day in John 5:39-40: "You search the Scriptures because you think that in them you have eternal life; it is these that testify about Me; and you are unwilling to come to Me so that you may have life." We go to the Word to see Jesus. Not to become brilliant theologians, although that may happen. Not to become the best speakers or writers in the world, although that may happen. Not to be used mightily by the Lord, although that too may happen. Paul speaks in Ephesians 1:10 of "the summing up of all things in Christ" and in Colossians 1:16-17, he says that "all things have been created through Him and for Him. He is before all things, and in Him all things hold together." Paul goes on to say in Colossians 1:18 that "He Himself will come to have first place in everything." It's all about Jesus.

I love the Bible because it is inspired by God. Peter said, "So we have the prophetic word made more sure, to which you do well to pay attention as to a lamp shining in a dark place, until the day dawns and the morning star arises in your hearts. But know this first of all, that no prophecy of Scripture is a matter of one's own interpretation, for no prophecy was ever made by an act of human will, but men moved by the Holy Spirit spoke from God" (2 Peter 1:19-21). I love these verses because they reassure me that the Bible I hold in my hands is more than words on a page. Donald Grey Barnhouse, a well-known theologian, was riding on the train one day. A student recognized him and said, "Dr. Barnhouse, how can I become a man of God like you?"

Dr. Barnhouse replied, "As long as you read those magazines more than the Word of God, you will know more about those magazines than you know about God." I love the Bible more than any other book in my library because it is the Word of God, not of man.

I love the Bible because it reveals the purpose of God. Every time I read it, I search for what the Lord wants to show me. God says in Isaiah 55:10-11, "For as the rain and the snow come down from heaven, and do not return there without watering the earth and making it bear and sprout, and furnishing seed to the sower and bread to the eater; so will My word be which goes forth from My mouth; It will not return to Me empty, without accomplishing what I desire, and without succeeding in the matter for which I sent it." I cannot be careless with the Word of God. I must regard the commands in the Word of God as imperatives, not as options. Whenever I sit down with the Word of God, I know that I am actually sitting down with the Lord. I must be ready to hear what He is saying to me.

I love the Bible because it is truth. In Jesus' prayer to the Father in John 17:17 He says, "Your word is truth." I know the world says we cannot know truth. Who is right? The world or Jesus? I choose the Word of God. I can hang my whole life on it. It is my reality in every situation. It is my light in a world of darkness. When I am in a dark time and having trouble understanding what is real and true, I open the Word of God. If necessary, I will wait on God for His answer.

I love the Bible because it is infinite. Paul says to "let the word of Christ richly dwell within you, with all wisdom teaching and admonishing one another with psalms and hymns and spiritual songs, singing with thankfulness in your hearts to God" (Colossians 3:16). The Greek word translated *richly* is *plousios,* meaning extravagant.[2] I can be extravagant with the Word of God because its riches are inexhaustible.

I love the Bible because it teaches me. Paul says in 2 Timothy 3:16-17 that God's Word is "profitable for teaching, for reproof, for correction, for training in righteousness; so that the man of God may be adequate, equipped for every good work." One day early on in my relationship with the Lord, I was feeling extremely rebellious because I was going through a very difficult time of suffering. In fact, I was feeling so angry about my trial, I was tempted to get in my car and drive off into the sunset. Thanks to the Holy Spirit in my life, I opened my Bible to 1 Peter 1:6-7: "In this you greatly rejoice, even though now for a little while, if necessary, you have been distressed by various trials, so that the proof of your faith, being more precious than gold which is perishable, even though tested by fire, may be found to result in praise and glory and honor at the revelation of Jesus Christ." I knew that this was God's Word for me that day. As I continued reading in 1 Peter about suffering, I felt as though every verse was written just for me. By the time I had finished reading 1 Peter, I had a completely different attitude about my own suffering. Rather than driving off into the sunset, I chose to "humble [myself] under the mighty hand of God, that He may exalt [me] at the proper time, casting all [my] anxiety on Him, because He cares for [me]" (1 Peter 5:6-7).

I love the Bible because it is the map for my life. "Your Word is a lamp to my feet and a light to my path" (Psalm 119:105). When my husband and I visited Scotland, we loved driving on the quaint roads—that is, until we encountered something new and puzzling to us: roundabouts. These circles of road would appear suddenly, replacing traffic lights and intersections, and required that we have a thorough knowledge of location and direction. Often, they presented three or four confusing choices, with roads sprouting from them like so many spokes of a wheel. My husband was in charge of the map, and I was in charge of the driving. I would call out, "A roundabout is coming!" and he would quickly consult the map and tell me which road to follow. We would enter the roundabout and keep driving in a circle until we saw our exit. Once we turned onto the correct road, we were on our way again. But driving on these roundabouts was surprisingly stressful at first because we had no plan and did not realize the importance of the map. Occasionally we drove in circles for a few minutes until we found our location on the map and our proper exit.

The Bible gives us guidance and direction in life. One day a repairman came to do some work at our Quiet Time Ministries Resource and Training Center. He began asking me what kind of church we were, and I explained that we were a ministry teaching devotion to God and His Word throughout the world. Then he asked me right out of the blue, "What do you believe about homosexuality?" My response shocked him. I said, "You know what? It doesn't really matter what I have to say or anyone else has to say. What really matters is what God says about homosexuality. Would you like to know what He has to say about it?" The man immediately responded, "Yes, definitely. I would like to know." I proceeded to show him Romans 1 and all that God had to say. He said, "You know what? You're the first person who has shown me what God says in the Bible."

Oh, how I love the Bible. It is the light in my darkness and holds the keys to unlock the door of truth in a lost and hurting world.

Thy Word is like a garden, Lord,
With flowers bright and fair;
And every one who seeks may pluck
A lovely cluster there.

Thy Word is like a deep, deep mine;
And jewels rich and rare
Are hidden in its mighty depths
For every searcher there.

Thy Word is like a starry host,
A thousand rays of light
Are seen to guide the traveler,
And make his pathway bright.

Thy Word is like an armory
Where soldiers may repair,
And find for life's long battle-day
All needful weapons there.

Oh, may I love Thy precious Word;
May I explore the mine;
May I its fragrant flowers glean;
May light upon me shine.

Oh, may I find my armor there;
Thy Word my trusty sword,
I'll learn to fight with every foe
The battle of the Lord.[3]

EDWIN HODDER

My Response

DATE:

KEY VERSE: "Nothing is perfect except your words. Oh, how I love them. I think about them all day long" (Psalm 119:96-97 TLB).

FOR FURTHER THOUGHT: How do you feel about the Bible today? Do you love the Word of God, and if so, why? What was your favorite reason to love the Word of God from today's reading? What was a new thought or application to you today?

MY RESPONSE:

THE SECRET GARDEN OF GOD'S WORD

*Receive and welcome the Word which
implanted and rooted [in your hearts]
contains the power to save your souls.*

JAMES 1:21 AMP

God's Word is your secret garden. Fellowshipping with God in His Word is like walking with God in the cool of the day in the garden of Eden. James encourages you to "receive and welcome the Word which implanted and rooted [in your hearts] contains the power to save your souls (James 1:21 AMP). The Message says it this way: "Let our gardener, God, landscape you with the Word, making a salvation-garden of your life." In this secret garden you can run, relax, and sit with the Lord. It is a place of delights that brings richness and joy and peace.

David describes his experience with God as a secret place: "How great is Your goodness, which You have stored up for those who fear You, which you have wrought for those who take refuge in You, before the sons of men! You hide them in the secret place of Your presence from the conspiracies of man; You keep them secretly in a shelter from the strife of tongues. Blessed be the LORD, for He has made marvelous His lovingkindness to me in a besieged city" (Psalm 31:19-21). Where can you run, where can you retreat, where can you hide, where can you experience God's presence regardless of what is facing you in life? The Bible. It is your secret garden where you meet with your Lord.

As so often happens, an unexpected turn of events can lead to a profound experience of God's presence. While visiting France one summer, my husband and I fled the oppressive heat in Paris on an air-conditioned bus tour to the castles of the Loire Valley. Château de Cheverny, Château de Chambord, and finally, the sixteenth-century home of Catherine de' Medici, Château de Chenonceau on the north bank of the Cher River. Not long after we arrived at Chenonceau, I broke away from the tour group and explored the Catherine de' Medici gardens on my own. I remember the peace and serenity that came over me as I first entered the walled garden area. Each bench along the pathway beckoned me to sit down and meditate on God and His creation. I thought about His sense of beauty. I pondered His divine order. And I realized His intimate care and concern over every detail of my life. The tour group saw floral symmetry, elevated terraces, and the Marques Tower. I saw the Lord. That is what happens when you know and love the Bible. It is as though you are in a secret garden that no one can touch. In that place you can stop, relax, and sit with the Lord. It is a secret place protected by God Himself.

Frances Hodgson Burnett's *The Secret Garden* follows a lonely little girl who discovers a secret walled garden as "the sweetest, most mysterious-looking place anyone could imagine." Having endured the recent loss of both her parents, she finds peace in this garden that was "different from any other place she had ever seen in her life...'How still it is!' she whispered. 'How still!'"[1]

In Psalm 46:10 (NIV) God says, "Be still and know that I am God." God is inviting you to a secret garden of intimacy and romance with Him.

- God's secret garden is possible. He invites you to experience Him firsthand, and He shows you how: by being still.

- God's secret garden is desirable. He wants you to know Him. Let His desire for you become your greatest desire too.

- God's secret garden is incredible. God's invitation to know that He is God implies a heart-to-heart relationship with Him.

- God's secret garden is unshakeable. Because He is God, your relationship with Him can never be taken away from you.

What does it mean to know God? The Hebrew word translated *know* is *yada* and implies an experience of the reality of His presence. Marvin Wilson, in his book *Our Father Abraham: Jewish Roots of the Christian Faith,* says, "In Hebrew thought, to 'know' something was to experience it, rather than merely to intellectualize it. To 'know' someone was to share an intimate personal relationship with that one. Thus the Hebrew verb *yada,* 'to know,' means to encounter, experience, and share in an intimate way."[2]

My understanding and experience of knowing God intimately became deep and meaningful when I began spending daily time alone with God. This quiet time became the most important part of my day. I learned to sit alone with my Bible open and my pen poised over a page in my journal to write insights as God opened up His Word to me.

How can you come to the garden of God's Word, be still, and know that He is God? Your quiet time with the Lord is the key. The most profound and well-written books of this world will not compare to one verse in the Bible that God has impressed on your heart in your time alone with Him. How can you develop this quiet time with the Lord? Here are some ideas to help you enjoy the secret garden of God's Word in your quiet time:

Have a firm resolve and commitment. Resolve to open God's Word every day. Commit to entering the palace of the Word instead of living in the small tent of this world. Feast on the food of the Word instead of the meager rations offered by the media. Make this daily commitment as an intentional decision ahead of time. Schedule it in your day.

Use a Bible reading plan. Live somewhere in the Bible each day by choosing a Bible reading plan. You may choose to use a devotional Bible, a one-year reading plan, or a Bible study. Follow your Bible reading plan every day to dig deeper and romance the Word.

Choose a good Bible translation. People often ask me which translation to use. Your choice will depend on your use. If you want a Bible for reading only, choose a thought-for-thought translation, such as the New International Version or the New Living Translation. If you plan to study God's Word, choose a word-for-word translation such as the New American Standard Bible or the English Standard Version. I also use paraphrases, such as The Message, The Living Bible, or J.B. Phillips' New Testament in Modern English as secondary Bibles. They are often helpful as commentaries on passages of Scripture.

Consult a good study Bible. A good study Bible includes contextual introductions for each book of the Bible, cross references, a concordance, and commentary study notes at the bottom of each page related to significant verses. Good study Bibles include *The New Inductive Study Bible,* the *NASB Zondervan Study Bible,* the *NIV Study Bible,* the *Ryrie Study Bible,* the *Life Application Bible, Nelson's NKJV Study Bible,* and the *Thompson Chain Reference Bible.*

Organize your quiet time materials. Going to the secret garden of God's Word in your quiet time includes organizing your Bible, notebook, devotional reading, prayer guides, pens, and pencils in one place.

Prepare to write. When you meet with God in the secret garden of His Word, He is going to teach you what is true and real. Write what God teaches you in a journal or notebook. Your writing may include significant verses, deep insights, poetry, stories, scriptural examples, word definitions, prayers, or life applications. I have a collection of notebooks and journals with such insights God has given me over the past 25 years. I like the *Quiet Time Notebook,* published by Quiet Time Ministries Press. Its six sections include pages for a journal, Bible study, prayer requests, application, reference study, and notes. Two additional sets of pages are also available for the notebook: Enriching Your Life of Prayer and Devotional Bible Study pages.

Prepare to interact with God's Word. Be prepared to mark in your Bible with a pen, pencil, and colored pencils. I like to highlight certain words that have become significant to me. I also underline key verses. Sometimes I write dates, names, or prayers next to certain verses. I write comments such as "awesome," "incredible," or "thank You, Lord" next to certain verses.

Ask God to prepare your heart. One of the best prayers in the Bible is "Open my eyes to see wonderful things in your Word" (Psalm 119:18 TLB). A prayer to ready the heart is Psalm 51:10 (ESV): "Create in me a clean heart, O God, and renew a right spirit within me." Be bold in your requests of God in the same way Moses was when he cried out, "I pray You, show me Your glory!" (Exodus 33:18). God loves that you thirst for Him, long for Him, and express your love for Him. He will answer your desire with Himself.

Set a time, a place, and a plan. Your journey to the secret garden of God's Word occurs in the context of a time, a place, and a plan. Choose a time when you can be alone with the Lord, find a place where you can experience undistracted devotion, and organize all your quiet time materials in that place. Even Jesus had a quiet time. Luke says that "Jesus Himself would often slip away to the wilderness and pray" (Luke 5:16). Use the P.R.A.Y.E.R. Quiet Time Plan:

Prepare your heart. James 4:8 encourages you to "draw near to God and He will draw near to you." Preparing your heart includes simple prayer, solitude, silence, journaling, and spiritual meditation.

Read and study God's Word. In Colossians 3:16, Paul encourages you to "let the word of Christ richly dwell within you." Reading and studying God's Word includes following your Bible reading plan, observation, interpretation, and application.

Adore God in prayer. In 1 Thessalonians 5:17, Paul says to "pray without ceasing." Adoring God in prayer may include adoration, confession, thanksgiving, supplication, writing prayer requests, praying for the world, and praying Scripture.

Yield yourself to God. In 1 Peter 5:6, Peter says, "Humble yourselves under the mighty hand of God, that He may exalt you at the proper time." Yielding yourself to God may include humility, submission, brokenness, and surrender to God.

Enjoy His presence. The psalmist says, "Delight yourself in the LORD; and He will give you the desires of your heart" (Psalm 37:4). Enjoying His presence may include such disciplines as practicing the presence of God, moment-by-moment prayer, extended times with the Lord, and personal retreats.

Rest in His love. Jesus said, "Come to Me, all who are weary and heavy-laden, and I will give you rest" (Matthew 11:28). Resting in His love includes sharing the life of Christ, discipleship, knowing the heart of Jesus, and bringing every part of your life to Him.

(For a better understanding and experience of the P.R.A.Y.E.R. Quiet Time Plan, read *Six Secrets to a Powerful Quiet Time,* Harvest House Publishers.)

Once you learn the devotional disciplines of the Quiet Time Plan, you will want to personalize them as the Lord leads you in your adventure with Him. This plan is flexible and can be a guideline whether you have ten minutes or two hours to spend with the Lord. It is a tool you can learn, practice, and develop over a lifetime. With the time, the place, and the plan, quiet time in the secret garden of God's Word is no longer a seemingly unattainable mystery but an exciting adventure. A quiet time is not an end in itself but a means to your desired goal: experiencing the great adventure of knowing God.

DATE:

KEY VERSE: "Receive and welcome the Word which implanted and rooted (in your hearts) contains the power to save your souls" (James 1:21 AMP).

FOR FURTHER THOUGHT: Will you make the choice to spend quiet time with Him each day to know and love Him through His Word? If so, you can know that nothing can touch that. A bad day can't touch that. A difficult job can't touch that. A difficult person in your life can't touch that. Terrorism can't touch that. Illness can't touch that. Death can't touch that. Nothing can touch that. Everything around you may change, but He will never change. You can count on that, and you can count on Him. In what way do you need the Lord in your life today?

MY RESPONSE:

THE TREASURE OF GOD'S WORD

But know this first of all, that no prophecy
of Scripture is a matter of one's own
interpretation, for no prophecy was ever
made by an act of human will, but men
moved by the Holy Spirit spoke from God.

2 PETER 1:20-21

The Bible you hold in your hands is an incredible treasure. In the Bible God is telling you what is on His mind and in His heart. It is His love letter to you. It is a handbook for your life. It is the ultimate how-to book. God is speaking to you personally in the Bible. Peter has made this clear in 2 Peter 1:20-21: "But know this first of all, that no prophecy of Scripture is a matter of one's own interpretation, for no prophecy was ever made by an act of human will, but men moved by the Holy Spirit spoke from God." The Bible is not merely static words on a page but the living Word of God.

I remember one day many years ago talking with a friend about the Bible. I had been in seminary for at least a year and was so excited at what

I was learning about the origin of the Bible. I told my friend about the journeys of Paul, his imprisonment, and his great love for the church as a background for his biblical letters. As I spoke, I saw a look of shock on her face, and I asked what was wrong. She replied, "Are you telling me that a real person actually wrote the words of Paul's letters?" I explained that it was God's Word, inspired by Him, but written through Paul in a real historical context. Then I asked her how she thought the Bible had been written. She thought the Bible had just appeared out of nowhere, mystically, without the involvement of human personality at all.

What is your concept of the Bible? Do you know what you hold in your hands when you open the pages of God's Word? A spiritual battle is being waged throughout the world for the truth of the Word of God. There are special interest, academic, and political groups tearing the Bible apart. When they have completed their work, they will have nothing of substance remaining. Some groups are eliminating the miraculous, denying the power and authority of God. Others are adding to the Bible in order to promote their own agendas, thoughts, and beliefs. Still others are choosing to give precedence to extrabiblical texts rather than the Bible. The battle over what constitutes the Word of God began in the early church, escalated during the Reformation, and is accelerating in the present age. In fact, countless people have sacrificed their lives that we might have a Bible in our hands so we might draw near to know and love God.

THE UNIQUENESS OF THE BIBLE

There is a reason why the Bible is the bestseller of all time. There is a reason why Bibles are marked up by men and women who have walked with God throughout their lives. There is a reason why Corrie ten Boom made every effort to carry her Bible with her into the horror of Ravensbruck concentration camp. There is a reason why a believing prison guard gave Bibles to every prisoner, knowing they were about to die. The Bible is more than a book. It is unique for several reasons.

The Bible has the power to change your life. Howard Hendricks says, "The Bible was written not to satisfy your curiosity but to help you conform to Christ's image. Not to make you a smarter sinner but to make you like the Savior. Not to fill your head with a collection of biblical facts but to transform your life."[1] The very deepest parts of our being are probed with the Great Physician's scalpel, yielding a perspective no human insight can provide. The Bible changes your life and does for you what you cannot do for yourself. "For the word of God is living and active and sharper than any two-edged sword, and piercing as far as the division of soul and spirit, of both joints and marrow, and able to judge the thoughts and intentions of the heart" (Hebrews 4:12).

The Bible is the revelation of God. When you open your Bible you will discover 66 books written over 1500 years of history by at least 40 authors. In other words, God revealed Himself and His ways to man progressively over a period of time. "God, after He spoke long ago to the fathers in the prophets in many portions and in many ways, in these last days has spoken to us in His Son" (Hebrews 1:1-2).

The Bible, God's Word, is written in a known human language. God chose to speak in language that human beings could understand. The original language of the Old Testament is ancient Hebrew with some Aramaic, and the original language of the New Testament is Koine Greek (the common language of the people in the first century) with some Aramaic phrases. Because the Bible was written in known languages, it could be translated into multitudes of other languages. In fact, it is being translated into new languages even at this very hour by skilled translators so that it may be read by people throughout the world. Glen C. Scorgie, in the book *The Challenge of Bible Translation,* helps us to not take this for granted:

> The divinely inspired Word first communicated through Hebrew and Greek language (and the ways of viewing life that those languages reflected) can now be meaningfully conveyed through other human languages as well. It is a great grace—and one to be celebrated by Christians—that divinely revealed truth is portable between linguistic systems and equally potent in its new dress.[2]

The Bible has a background and context in history. The revelation of God is given within a historical context; that is, God sent His message through many authors, each with his own personality, expressing his own cultural background. J. Robertson McQuilken makes this note in his book *Understanding and Applying the Bible:*

> The Bible is revelation in history, unlike the teachings of many religions. Some religions are rooted in mythology, such as Shintoism or Hinduism. Others were founded by a historic individual, but large elements of religious teachings today are mythological, such as Buddhism. In contrast to those, Scripture is rooted in history and claims to be a historical document, the record of God's self-revelation to man. As such, we must understand it in the context of its history.[3]

This historical context allows for an accurate study of cultures, historical events, and interpretation.

The Bible is written by God and inspired by God. Although it was written over a great time span by many authors, the Bible presents a distinct unity in thought and belief. The Bible is inspired by God. This means He is the author, the single source affirming the authenticity and trustworthiness of the entire biblical canon. Josh McDowell challenged a representative of *The Great Books of the Western World* to consider just ten authors, all from one walk of life, one generation, one place, one mood, and one language, and just one controversial subject. He then asked the representative, "Would the authors agree with one another?" The man admitted, "No." Josh then presented the uniformity of thought in the biblical text. Days later, the man committed his life to Christ.[4]

The Bible is unlike any other book. Imagine that God purposed in His heart and mind to give us something tangible in a language we can understand so that we may know and love Him. It is a miracle that we can even have such a treasure. All earthly possessions erode over time, but not the Word of God. It is eternal.

THE BIBLE IS INSPIRED

"All Scripture is inspired by God and profitable for teaching, for reproof, for correction, for training in righteousness; so that the man of God may be adequate, equipped for every good work" (2 Timothy 3:16). The Greek word for *inspired* is *theopneustos* and literally means

"God-breathed," meaning that the origin is God, not man. The Holy Spirit so worked through the human writers, despite different styles and personalities, that the written Word of God is authoritative, trustworthy, and free from error in the original autographs.[5]

THE BIBLE IS INERRANT

To say that the Bible is inerrant is to say that it tells the truth and is free from error. Different styles of writing and different views of the same event do not constitute error. Paul Enns says the following about inerrancy of Scripture:

> When correctly understood, it means that the Bible speaks accurately in all its statements, whether theological matters, the creation account, history, geography, or geology. It does, however, allow for variety in details concerning the same account; it does not demand rigidity of style. In all the Bible's statements it is accurate and in accord with the truth.[6]

THE BIBLE IS INFALLIBLE

In the fall of 1978, an international summit conference of evangelical leaders produced the Chicago Statement on Biblical Inerrancy, which includes this sentence: "*Infallible* signifies the quality of neither misleading nor being misled and so safeguards in categorical terms the truth that Holy Scripture is a sure, safe, and reliable rule and guide in all matters."[7] It is dependable as the object of your faith and the sure foundation to give you confidence to do what it says.

SOLA SCRIPTURA

Sola scriptura implies that the Bible is the sole authority for one's belief. *Sola scriptura,* the Latin phrase meaning "Scripture alone," was coined by the theologians of the Reformation to point out that only the Bible has the right to command the beliefs and actions of people. It is the final court of appeals for all doctrine and practice, is infallible, and is all that is needed to know God's truth. This contrasts with the belief that an additional teaching authority such as the church, a religious guru, or a governing body is required to understand the Bible.

The principle of *sola scriptura* reached its zenith in the early sixteenth century as Martin Luther nailed his "95 Theses" to the church door at Wittenberg. Following a powerful spiritual experience centered on Romans 1:18, "the just shall live by faith," Luther held that the sole authority for Christian experience was the Word of God, in contrast to the teachings of the church of his day. Luther was arrested and brought before the authorities of the church, who demanded that he recant all his teachings. He prayed all night. When he returned, he spoke with such force and power about the truth of God's Word and the sole authority of God's Word that the room was silent. He said the following: "Unless I am convicted of error by the testimony of Scriptures or (since I put no trust in the unsupported authority of the Pope or of councils, since it is plain that they have erred and often contradicted themselves) by manifest reasoning I stand convicted by the Scriptures to which I have appealed, and my conscience is taken captive by God's word, I cannot and will not recant anything, for to act against conscience is neither safe for us nor open to us. On this I take my stand. I can do no other. God help me. Amen." Luther was not executed that day. The ongoing work of the Bible continued, and ultimately it made its way into the hands of the people.

THE CANON

The word *canon,* when used in connection with the Bible, describes the collection of the 66 books comprising the inspired Word of God. It is the Bible as we know it today. Whereas the Greek origin is *kanon,* the Hebrew word is *qaneh,* the word for a measuring rod. The Council of Jamnia in AD 90 is generally considered the occasion when the Old Testament canon was publicly recognized. Criteria for the Old Testament canon included internal evidence of divine authorship, the writer as spokesman for God, and historical accuracy. The process of the recognition and collection of the New Testament canon took place in the first centuries of the Christian church. Criteria for the New Testament canon included apostolicity, acceptance, content, and inspiration. At no time were the councils causing inspiration; they were simply recognizing it. Therefore, the Bible you hold in your hands is complete and what God intended to say to you in written form. That is why it has often been called His love letter to you.

THE BIBLE IS RELIABLE

The reliability of the Bible depends on its accuracy. As original manuscripts began to show wear over time, they were reverently copied by ancient scribes, word by word, character by character, to produce exact copies of each book of the Bible. From the days of Ezra, the tradition of copying text included quite tedious procedures, such as counting letters in a book and noting middle letters in the text. The discovery of the Dead Sea Scrolls in 1947 was the defining moment in modern history for substantiating biblical accuracy. From that archaeological find, the oldest manuscripts of the Bible could be compared to the subsequent manuscripts throughout history, thus confirming textual accuracy.

THE HISTORY OF THE PRINTED BIBLE

Imagine a world without a written Bible. For many centuries, the Bible was only in the hands of the church leaders, its sole interpreters and dictators of the beliefs and actions of the people. How did the Bible move from ancient writing on papyrus to the printed word we have today? The word *Bible* comes from the Greek word *biblion,* which in turn comes from the word *biblos,* another word for the plant that is the source for papyrus, the writing material of the ancient world.[8] Other writing materials in the ancient world included parchment and leather. Because parchment was more durable than papyrus, most of our Old Testament and New Testament manuscripts are parchment. The originals were most likely written on papyrus (see 2 John 12).

Throughout the centuries, various translators took the available collections of the Old and New Testaments and translated them into the languages of the day. One of the earliest translations was the Latin Vulgate by Jerome in the fourth century. Not until Gutenberg published the first Bible in 1452 were these translations duplicated and available to the masses. Gutenberg printed 30 copies on parchment using some 46,000 wood blocks of movable type. During the next 50 years, 100 editions of his two-volume Latin Bible were published.

Erasmus published the first Greek New Testament with a definitive fourth edition in 1527.

With the Bible in Latin or Greek, the Word of God was not readily available to those who could read only English. Therefore, people relied on the church to interpret Scripture for them. Unfortunately, the church often served its own interests and created many religious ideas that did not have their origin in Scripture.

John Wycliffe, an Oxford theologian in the late 1300s, was burdened for people to have their own Bibles so that they might order their lives by the truth of its words. His passion was to give the people the Word of God in their own language. He developed an English version of the Bible translated directly from the Latin Vulgate, but this new translation was a direct threat to the church. In 1415, the Council of Constance condemned the writings of Wycliffe, and in 1428, his bones were dug up and burned.

William Tyndale (1494–1536) is considered to be the true father of the English Bible because his English translation was derived from the original Hebrew and Greek, and it was printed rather than copied.[9] Tyndale vowed that the plowboy would know more about Scripture than the priests. His desire was to promote Christian growth and effectiveness in the lives of all the people. We see this in his statement in the Old English style: "that the sainctes might have all thinges necessarie to worke and minister with all, to the edifyinge of the body of Christ."[10] Tyndale realized his dream of an English translation of the Bible by leaving his beloved country, England, and traveling to Germany to complete the work. Tyndale barely escaped from Cologne when his work became known and was forbidden by authorities. The first printing of his New Testament in English was completed in Worms in 1526. Within a month, copies made their way to England, smuggled in barrels and other containers of merchandise. The church was incensed and burned as many copies as it could find. Tyndale continued his work of translation and printing until Emperor Charles V declared him a heretic and condemned him to be executed. William Tyndale was strangled to death and then burned at the stake in 1536. His last words were, "Lord, open the King of England's eyes."[11]

A Bible of Your Own

It is a wondrous privilege that you and I can have our own Bibles to open, read, and study whenever we choose. Thousands of Bibles are available in many languages throughout the world because of the sacrifice of such men as Luther, Wycliffe, and Tyndale. And now, near the end of our first week together, it is important for you to think about your own Bible. You may have study Bibles, commentaries, and other resources to help you grow. However, the most important tool in your life is a Bible that you can read, live in, and grow to know and love. Choose a Bible that has an easily readable type and font size. Choose a soft leather edition if you can afford it. You will want a size that you can carry around. Have a good supply of pens and pencils to use for marking in your Bible. Then, get ready for the adventure of your life as you take advantage of the opportunity God has given to you through such servants as Tyndale and Wycliffe, and open the pages of your Bible.

The Treasure You Have in Your Hands

You may hardly be able to imagine that holding the Bible in your own hands was once considered a crime. But such was the case for people like Tyndale and Wycliffe. Could you imagine your church calling you in front of the board to ask you to lay aside the authority of God's Word in your life? But some forces in the world today would keep you from opening your Bible in public. Paul describes our spiritual battle in Ephesians 6:12-13:

> Our struggle is not against flesh and blood, but against the rulers, against the powers, against the world forces of this darkness, against the spiritual forces of wickedness in the heavenly places. Therefore, take up the full armor of God, so that you will be able to resist in the evil day, and having done everything, to stand firm.

Paul ends this section on spiritual warfare by telling you to take up the "sword of the Spirit, which is the word of God" (Ephesians 6:17). Oh, how desperately we need men and women who have hearts like Luther's and Tyndale's, spiritual warriors willing to stand against the tide and fight for the truth of God's Word! Think about the transmission of the texts down through the years and those who risked and actually gave their lives so that you might hold a Bible in your hands. It gives great cause for thanks to a gracious God, who would give such a gift to you. Now the question is, will you take advantage of the great opportunity to open the pages of His Word and hear what He has to say to you? If so, then you are God's man or God's woman for such a time as this.

My Response

DATE:

KEY VERSE: "But know this first of all, that no prophecy of Scripture is a matter of one's own interpretation, for no prophecy was ever made by an act of human will, but men moved by the Holy Spirit spoke from God" (2 Peter 1:20-21).

FOR FURTHER THOUGHT: Why is God's Word such a treasure? How do people in the church feel about the Word compared to the convictions of men like Wycliffe, Tyndale, and Luther? How has today's reading changed your own feeling about God's Word? What needs to change in your own life for you to appreciate the importance and value of the Word?

MY RESPONSE:

Day Six

QUIET TIME— WEEK ONE: THE DIVINE ROMANCE

Prepare Your Heart

Martin Luther was born in Eisleben, Germany in 1483. During his studies to become a lawyer, he was almost struck by lightning. This near-death experience so affected him that he decided to join the Augustinian friars, and his superiors guided him to study theology at the university in Wittenberg, where he eventually became a professor.

Luther was an unusual man in his day. Theologians were encouraged to study the writings of men, not the Bible. The Bible was not readily available, not even to those with seminary degrees. Luther remarked that one of his fellow professors did not even own a Bible. Luther's first view of a Bible was in a library in Erfurt when he was 20 years old. What excitement he experienced when he first entered the Augustinian monastery overseen by Johann Staupitz, a great lover of the Bible. Because of his firm belief in direct study of the Word of God, Staupitz ensured that each novice was given a red leather Bible. Novices were encouraged to read and study their Bibles. Luther did exactly that and fell in love with God's Word. In fact, he knew the Bible so well that it is said he knew what was on every page and could locate any passage of Scripture he heard. He spoke of his time in the Word this way: "For some years now, I have read through the Bible twice every year. If you picture the Bible to be a mighty tree and every word a little branch, I have shaken every one of these branches because I wanted to know what it was and what it meant." He especially loved the Word because it answered the problems of life and was new to him every day. He loved the joy of discovery. God used Martin Luther in a powerful way to teach that the only authority for belief is the Bible. Luther's last writing, found on a slip of paper by his bed after he died, was a word of praise for the Bible and an appeal for others to read it with a humble spirit.

As you begin your quiet time today, read Psalm 1. As you think about these words, think about Luther and his picture of the Bible as a mighty tree that we need to shake in order to discover what is there. Do you have the kind of love for the Bible we see in Psalm 1 and in the life of Martin Luther? Write a prayer to the Lord expressing all that is on your heart today.

Read and Study God's Word

Josiah became king of Judah at the age of eight. In 2 Kings 23:25 we learn that "before him there was no king like him who turned to the LORD with all his heart and with all his soul and with all his might, according to all the law of Moses; nor did any like him arise after him." There was a secret to Josiah's life: When he discovered the Word of God, he wholeheartedly embraced it. Read 2 Kings 22:1–23:3 and write out what is most significant to you about Josiah and the Word of God.

Write out 2 Kings 23:3, word for word, in the space provided, thinking about all that it says.

As you think about Josiah and his embrace of God's Word in 2 Kings 23:3, are you willing to make that same kind of move toward the Bible? What will it take for you to embrace it with your whole heart? Write out your commitment.

ADORE GOD IN PRAYER

> Deal bountifully with Your servant,
> that I may live and keep Your word.
> Open my eyes, that I may behold
> wonderful things from Your law.
> PSALM 119:17-18

YIELD YOURSELF TO GOD

Meditate on the following quotes by Luther:

The Bible is the proper book for men. There the truth is distinguished from error far more clearly than anywhere else, and one finds something new in it every day. For twenty-eight years, since I became a doctor, I have now constantly read and preached the Bible; and yet I have not exhausted it but find something new in it every day.

You should diligently learn the Word of God and by no means imagine that you know it. Let him who is able to read take a psalm in the morning, or some other chapter of Scripture, and study it for a while. This is what I do. When I get up in the morning, I pray and recite the Ten Commandments, the Creed, and the Lord's Prayer with the children, adding any one of the psalms. I do this only to keep myself well acquainted with these matters, and I do not want to let the mildew of the notion grow that I know them well enough. The devil is a greater rascal than you think he is. You do as yet not know what sort of fellow he is and what a desperate rogue you are. His definite design is to get you tired of the Word and in this way to draw you away from it. This is his aim.

He who would correctly and profitably read Scripture should see to it that he finds Christ in it; then he finds life eternal without fail. On the other hand, if I do not so study and understand Moses and the prophets as to find that Christ came from heaven for the sake of my salvation, became man, suffered, died, was buried, rose, and ascended into heaven so that through Him I enjoy reconciliation with God, forgiveness of all my sins, grace, righteousness, and life eternal, then my reading in Scripture is of no help whatsoever to my salvation. I may, of course, become a learned man by reading and studying Scripture and preach what I have acquired; yet all this would do me no good whatever.

ENJOY HIS PRESENCE

Have you engaged in this great romance of God and His Word, the Bible? Have you fallen in love with your Lord, who spoke all the words contained in it? Think about all you have learned today from the lives of Luther and Josiah. Josiah and all the people made a commitment to the Lord, a covenant. After that covenant, they made radical changes so they could follow hard after God. They got rid of the things in their lives that they were worshipping instead of God. Now is the time to lay aside whatever is weighing you down and keeping you from wholeheartedly opening your Bible and following God. Write a prayer of commitment and resolve to the Lord about His Word in your life.

REST IN HIS LOVE

"Oh, how I love your law! I think about it all day long" (Psalm 119:97 NLT).

Notes—Week One

EMBRACE THE ROMANCE

Days 7-12

THE MIRROR OF GOD'S WORD

*For now we see in a mirror dimly,
but then face to face; now I know in
part, but then I will know fully just
as I also have been fully known.*

1 CORINTHIANS 13:12

The Bible shows you the truth about God and the truth about you. It is a mirror reflecting God's ways and character so that you may know and love Him. Paul told the church at Corinth, "For now we see in a mirror dimly, but then face to face; now I know in part, but then I will know fully just as I also have been fully known." This is the challenge: to live in the now, where we see dimly, until we get to eternity, where we will see all things clearly. The secret is to look in the mirror. This week, as we continue our journey to know and love the Bible, we want to explore a very important perspective of the Bible—its ability to act as a mirror, to give us a clear view of reality, the truth in any situation.

James likens the Word of God to a mirror:

> Be doers of the word, and not hearers only, deceiving yourselves. For if anyone is a hearer of the word and not a doer, he is like a man observing his natural face in a mirror; for he observes himself, goes away, and immediately forgets what kind of man he was. But he who looks into the perfect law of liberty and continues in it, and is not a forgetful hearer but a doer of the work, this one will be blessed in what he does (James 1:22-25 NKJV).

In every situation of life, James insists that you look into the mirror, discover what is true and real, and respond in sincere devotion.

We have a love-hate relationship with mirrors. Why? Because mirrors tell the truth. Years ago, I remember walking into a women's lounge at a restaurant. An older woman walked up to the mirror, looked in the mirror, looked at me, and exclaimed, "Don't ever get old. It's terrible!" That woman did not feel happy about what she saw in the mirror. I thought she looked terrific, but she didn't think so. However, mirrors can show you many wonderful things. I remember the first time my little niece, then three years old, walked past a floor-to-ceiling mirror. She studied herself, perhaps for the first time. At first, she quickly looked away. Then she got up the courage to look again, finally just staring at herself, examining every detail. She was seeing the truth about what she looked like. It was a new and exciting experience for her.

What is the great value of having a mirror from God? Have you ever suffered a loss and concluded that life or ministry is over? Have you ever felt that your loss is so large, you will never recover? Has your loss plunged you into despair and discouragement? Paul addresses the issue of affliction from an eternal viewpoint:

> We do not lose heart, but though our outer man is decaying, yet our inner man is being renewed day by day. For momentary, light affliction is producing for us an eternal weight of glory far beyond all comparison, while we look not at the things which are seen, but at the things which are not seen; for the things which are seen are temporal, but the things which are not seen are eternal (2 Corinthians 4:16-18).

Most people only see what is in front of their eyes in the present, but the mirror of the Word will help you see all the way to eternity. If you do not see your situation in the mirror of the Word, you will see it incorrectly. You will make false conclusions about your situation. And you will act incorrectly based on those false conclusions. You can even become downhearted and fall into despair. But what if you had another view, an eternal view, that is more true than what you see in the here and now? Wouldn't you like to have that new view of your own circumstance? A view from the Lord Himself? Remember, the Lord knows you completely—your circumstances, your challenges, your weaknesses, your strengths, your joys, your sorrows. He has the perfect view from eternity for you, and the true perspective is often completely different from what you see right now. The secret is to look in the mirror.

When you look in the mirror of the Word, you will see yourself. What you see is both humbling and magnificent. Job, as he thought about God and man, said, "What is man, that you make so much of him, and that you set your heart on him?" (Job 7:17 ESV). In contrast, the psalmist said, "I will give thanks to You, for I am fearfully and wonderfully made; wonderful are Your works, and my soul knows it very well" (Psalm 139:14). I struggled with a poor self-image in grade school and into high school. When I became a Christian and began reading the Bible, I gained a whole new view of myself. I saw that God loved me. That He designed me and made me unique. He changed my whole view of myself and gave me a new confidence in life.

When you look in the mirror of the Word, you will see God's designs for your life. The Word encourages you that God has a plan and a purpose for your life. "'For I know the plans that I have for you,' declares the Lord, 'plans for welfare and not for calamity to give you a future and a hope'" (Jeremiah 29:11). Countless times in my life, I thought all was lost. I thought my life was over and I had no hope. Then I discovered the truth of God's plans and purposes in Jeremiah 29:11. I saw the truth of Philippians 1:6: "For I am confident of this very thing, that He who began a good work in you will perfect it until the day of Christ Jesus." God's promises in the mirror of the Bible encourage me that it is always too soon to give up.

When you look in the mirror of the Word, you will see your potential in

Christ. You will see the face of Christ, and what you see will make you more like Him. Paul says, "We all, with unveiled face, beholding as in a mirror the glory of the Lord, are being transformed into the same image from glory to glory, just as from the Lord, the Spirit" (2 Corinthians 3:18). I have always been an idea person. And some of those ideas have been so big that I have thought I could never attempt such things. But then I look in the mirror of the Bible and see such promises as "I can do all things through Him who strengthens me" (Philippians 4:13), "It is no longer I who live, but Christ lives in me" (Galatians 2:20), and God "is able to do far more abundantly beyond all that we ask or think, according to the power that works within us" (Ephesians 3:20). What I see in the mirror of the Bible encourages me to dream big and dare to do great and mighty things in the power and strength of God.

When you look in the mirror of the Word, you will see God's character. You will understand His heart and His ways, and you will experience intimacy with Him. Moses prayed, "Let me know Your ways that I may know You, so that I may find favor in Your sight" (Exodus 33:13). When I look into the mirror of the Bible, I always ask, what can I learn about God today? I remember being in a difficult circumstance and feeling so alone. I began studying the first three chapters of Revelation, which contain seven letters from Jesus to the seven churches of western Asia Minor. One of the phrases Jesus repeated over and over in those letters was "I know." The truth dawned on me that He knows my situation too. I realized I am not alone. He is with me.

When you look in the mirror of the Word, you will find the good news of eternal life. Regardless of the greatness of your sin, forgiveness is available. That's the good news of the gospel. Paul said, "For I am not ashamed of the gospel, for it is the power of God for salvation to everyone who believes, to the Jew first and also to the Greek" (Romans 1:16 ESV). You will discover when you look in the mirror that "God so loved the world, that He gave His only begotten Son, that whoever believes in Him shall not perish, but have eternal life" (John 3:16). Jesus died for your sins because of His love for you. You can receive forgiveness of sins because He paid the price with His death on the cross. By His grace, He offers you the gift of forgiveness.

When you look in the mirror of the Word, you will see His promises. The promises of God enable us to experience His nature. "As we know Jesus better, his divine power gives us everything we need for living a godly life. He has called us to receive his own glory and goodness! And by that same mighty power, he has given us all of his rich and wonderful promises" (2 Peter 1:3-4 NLT). Eugene Peterson calls the promises of God "tickets to participation in the life of God" (2 Peter 1:4 MSG). You can count on the promises of God. When God promises something, He will do it. When He says He will never leave you or forsake you (see Hebrews 13:7), you can count on that. When you look into the mirror of the Bible, you will see promises on every page. Grasp hold of the promises. Trust the promises. Believe the promises. And live out those promises.

Sometimes I don't feel significant. I don't feel loved. I don't feel forgiven. I don't feel as if I have hope. At those times, I want to run away. That picture of my life seems true and real to me. And if I stopped there, I would fall into despair. But then I look in the mirror of God's Word. And I see the real picture, the true picture. Feelings are like the caboose of a train that must be hitched to the engine of God's Word.

James Cash Penney opened a chain of retail stores in the late 1920s. After some time, his company went public. Six days later, the stock market crashed, and he lost everything. He was so devastated that he checked himself into a sanitarium. One night he went to bed in such despair that he was certain he would not wake up the next day. And yet he did. Wandering the hallways, he heard a group singing, "God Will Take Care of You." Those words spoke to his heart, and he was instantly a changed man. He joined that meeting and listened to the words of the hymn, the Scripture, and the prayers. A huge burden was lifted from him that day. He asked God to take care of him and knew that He would, regardless of what happened. He went home and spent more time with his wife and children.

At the age of 56 he had to start over, and yet God gave him the strength to put one foot in front of the other. He never regained the wealth he once possessed, but within ten years, he was once again prosperous. Near the end of his life, he began losing his eyesight. He was heard to say, "My sight is gone, but my vision is better than ever." In

1971 he died at the age of 95. J.C. Penney was one of those rare hearts who knew how to look into the mirror of the Word of God.

The secret is to look in the mirror.

My Response

DATE:

KEY VERSE: "For now we see in a mirror dimly, but then face to face; now I know in part, but then I will know fully just as I also have been fully known" (1 Corinthians 13:12).

FOR FURTHER THOUGHT: In what way is God's Word a mirror? What will you see when you look in the mirror of God's Word? What do you need to see today as you look in the mirror of God's Word? Can you say with James Cash Penney, "My sight is gone, but my vision is better than ever"? Record your thoughts today. Look in the mirror of God's Word, and you will see as you have never seen before. Regardless of how deep your trouble is or how wrecked your life seems, if you can just reach through the fog of today's trial, look in the mirror, grasp the vision of eternal things, and embrace them as your own, you can march on in the direction of your eternal destiny. It is not easy, but it is possible. The more you look, the more you will see. (Weeks three and four will concentrate on learning how to look in the mirror of the Word.)

MY RESPONSE:

Day Eight

THE TRUTH
ABOUT TRUTH

Your word is truth.
JOHN 17:17

God determines truth, and we discover it. You can know what is true because God has spoken, and what He says is true. When Jesus prayed for His disciples, He dedicated them to the Father by means of the truth. He prayed to the Father, "Your word is truth" (John 17:17). Absolute truth is found in only one place: the Word of God. Yesterday we saw that the Bible is a mirror that shows us the truth. Today we want to explore the importance of truth for our lives. Thinking about this is especially important because we live in a culture that doesn't believe in absolute truth, doesn't know the truth, and cannot reflect the truth.

I am deeply motivated by truth. Jesus said, "I am the way, and the truth, and the life; no one comes to the Father but through Me" (John 14:6). I surrendered my life to Jesus because I realized if He is the truth, to live for anything else is to live for a lie. I want to know the truth, the objective reality, in every situation.

When my husband and I visited Universal Studios in southern

California, we took the tram tour of all the different movie sets. One set in particular taught me a deep spiritual lesson. The tram traveled through what appeared to be a small town with storefronts, streets, and sidewalks. The stunning reality became clear when the tram continued on behind the town. Everyone gasped when they saw the town was painted boards held up by wood supports. You can't live in a town that isn't real. And a life that is built on a lie ultimately has no substance. The secret is found in the words of Jesus: "You will know the truth, and the truth will make you free" (John 8:32).

The first time my husband and I visited Rome, we immediately sought out the Roman Forum because it was not simply the heart of an ancient city but the center of the world at the time of Jesus of Nazareth. From the origins of the empire under Augustus in 31 BC, and for nearly 500 years thereafter, Roman emperors, deified as gods, ruled most of the civilized world. And yet as my husband and I drank in our first look of the Arch of Septimius Severus, the Basilica Julia, the Curia Hostilia, the Palatine Hill, and off in the distance, the grand Colosseum, our first impression was not of awe and grandeur but sadness. Piazzas, arches, columns, temples, statues—all in ruins. The Foro Romano was nothing more than ruin and rubble.

What moves a thriving culture to ruins? The Roman Empire fell in AD 476, the consequence of its own belief system, which was based on the finite rather than the infinite, relativism rather than truth, deified emperors rather than the one true God. The future of a culture rests on whether its foundation is built on truth. Jesus referred to this in Matthew 7:24-28 (NIV):

> Everyone who hears these words of mine and puts them into practice is like a wise man who built his house on the rock. The rain came down, the streams rose, and the winds blew and beat against that house; yet it did not fall, because it had its foundation on the rock. But everyone who hears these words of mine and does not put them into practice is like a foolish man who built his house on sand. The rain came down, the streams rose, and the winds blew and beat against that house, and it fell with a great crash.

Only a life or culture built on the truth of God's Word will stand.

THE INDICTMENT

We live in a society where many believe absolute truth is nonexistent or irrelevant, reflecting a worldview often called *postmodernism*. This worldview includes the claim that your truths are your truths, and my truths are my truths. Many have a buffet belief system, sampling a little bit of this and a little bit of that. The individual becomes the standard and selects beliefs and convictions based on whatever seems right. The chilling reality is that the buffet belief system has crept into the modern church. Some no longer recognize the distinction between right and wrong or see the relevance of truth for their lives. Only 45 percent of professing Christians who attend church regularly ever open their Bibles outside of their time in church. A study by George Barna in 2002 revealed that 75 percent of Americans age 18 to 35 and 68 percent of evangelicals did not believe in absolute truth. When taken to the extreme, denying or ignoring absolute truth makes one either a practical athiest or a practical agnostic.

Allan Bloom says this in the introduction of *The Closing of the American Mind:*

> There is one thing a professor can be absolutely certain of: almost every student entering the university believes, or says he believes, that truth is relative. The danger every student has been taught to fear from truth is not error but intolerance. They have been taught to believe that relativism is necessary to openness. Openness is the call of the moment.[1]

People who promote this kind of extreme tolerance contend that all beliefs are equally valid. Truth is not called *fact* but *belief* according to the world. People often say, "Whatever you believe is right for you." In one cartoon, a minister is marrying a couple, and the groom is slouching with his hands in his pockets. The caption shows the minister saying, "No, no, no! You're supposed to say "I do," not "Whatever!""

Relativity has replaced reality. Most people seem to be living in that Universal Studios small town that has no substance. The absence of truth and the "whatever" belief system has resulted in moral chaos with everyone doing "whatever."

A driver was following a car sporting the bumper sticker, "If it feels good, do it." At a stoplight the guy couldn't resist the temptation, pressed the gas pedal, and bumped the car ahead of him. The driver's head spun around, and he angrily got out of his car. "What are you doing?" the driver asked. The guy responded, "It felt good, so I did it."

Ravi Zacharias states that "An absolute is basically an unchanging point of reference by which all other changes are measured...Truth... can exist only if there is an objective standard by which to measure it. That objective, unchanging absolute is God."[2]

THE VERDICT

> Therefore Pilate said to Him, "So you are a king?"
>
> Jesus answered, "You say correctly that I am a king. For this I have been born, and for this I have come into the world, to testify to the truth. Everyone who is of the truth hears My voice."
>
> Pilate said to Him, "What is truth?" (John 18:37-38)

What is truth? The Greek word for truth is *aletheia,* which means "the reality lying at the basis of an appearance, the manifested veritable essence of a matter."[3]

Truth begins with God. Truth is that which corresponds to objective reality. And what is objective reality? God. If something outside the realm of time corresponds with reality, it is the measure for all that is true. God is the measure of what is true. He determines what is true. He has no beginning and no end. He is eternal. He is unchangeable. He cannot lie. If you wish to know whether a line is straight, you hold a ruler next to it. If you wish to draw a straight line, you use a ruler. The ruler for life, the measure of all that is true and real, is God Himself. If in fact God has spoken, what He says in His Word is the measure for all that is true and real. The only way you can know whether something is true is by looking at what God says in His Word.

Truth belongs to God. It is His truth. The Bible is not something that becomes your truth. It *is* the truth. So many in the world today say that Christianity is your truth and I have my truth. Truth is not determined by anyone who wants to determine it, as the world believes. Truth is revealed by God and discovered by those who seek it out in God's Word.

Truth is revealed by God. God has spoken through *general revelation* to all mankind through nature, through providential control, and through conscience. The psalmist says, "The heavens are telling of the glory of God; and their expanse is declaring the work of His hands. Day to day pours forth speech, and night to night reveals knowledge" (Psalm 19:1-2). I like to think of general revelation as God's multimedia. All you need to do is look at the stars on a clear night, and you have a multimedia presentation by God declaring His majestic glory. But God also speaks through *special revelation* in Jesus Christ and through His Word, the Bible. In Hebrews 1:1-3 we see that "God, after He spoke long ago to the fathers in the prophets in many portions and in many ways, in these last days has spoken to us in His Son, whom He appointed heir of all things, through whom also He made the world." Second Peter 1:21 says, "No prophecy was ever made by an act of human will, but men moved by the Holy Spirit spoke from God." That is why the Bible is called God's Word.

Truth depends on God, not on belief. Therefore, not all beliefs are valid. Only what is true is valid and real. The strength and sincerity of one's belief does not make it true. Only what corresponds with reality is true. Therefore what you believe is important, not how strong and great your ability to believe. God exists—that is a fact. My belief does not cause Him to exist. He exists whether I believe it or not. God's Word is true—that is a fact. Whether you believe it or not does not change the truth of His Word. I often think of the example of a plane with no wings and no engine. My sincere belief that the plane will fly does not make it true.

Truth finds its expression in the gospel. God saves men and women through Christ. The gospel flows through lives that are founded on truth and that demonstrate truth. In John 14:6 Jesus says, "I am the way, and the truth, and the life; no one comes to the Father but through

Me." One of His claims is that He is the truth. There is only one way to handle this claim of Jesus: by believing in Him.

Truth is the authority for your belief. Every person must answer some questions about his or her life. What is the origin of life? What is the meaning of life? How can I know right and wrong? What happens to me when I die? What is the meaning of history? Is the universe following a plan? In answering these questions, you want answers that correspond with reality. You want to know truth. The truth in the Bible possesses the ultimate authority to command your beliefs and actions. Jesus said, "Heaven and earth will pass away, but My words will not pass away" (Mark 13:31 ESV). "The grass withers, the flowers fade, but the Word of our God shall stand forever" (Isaiah 40:8 TLB). Paul tells us in 2 Timothy 3:16 that "all Scripture is inspired by God and profitable for teaching, for reproof, for correction, for training in righteousness." And Jesus declares to us that "Scripture cannot be broken" (John 10:35).

Truth in the Bible is relevant for your life. You are accountable to God's truth as it commands your response. Jesus is inviting you to a relationship that has eternal significance. If what He says is true, your life depends upon it. He makes an exclusive claim, and He asks for a response that determines your eternal destiny—life or death. How essential is truth? I had the opportunity to play golf on a famous course in northern California, where the eighth hole stretches 250 yards off the tee toward a treacherous cliff. Standing on the tee, the cliff and its drop to the ocean are hidden by the slope of the fairway. The caddies tell a horrific story of a couple who jumped into their golf cart after hitting their drives and drove merrily on their way, ignoring the warning sign about the cliff. They kept driving forward until they drove straight off the cliff. Was the truth of the cliff and its warning sign relevant for those unfortunate golfers? Absolutely.

Truth guides your life. What will be the result of truth from God's Word in your life? What you believe determines who you are. Who you are determines how you live. And how you live determines the direction of your life. God desires for us to be people of conviction. A conviction is a strong belief that results in a corresponding action. David, the man after God's own heart, was a man of conviction—he was always saying "I will do this" and "I will do that." That's not legalism, that's love! Paul too was a man of conviction: I do all things for the sake of the gospel (1 Corinthians 9:19-23). How do you carry out a conviction based on God's Word? By faith. Take God at His Word.

On Wednesday, March 5, 1997, Dr. Bill Bright, founder of Campus Crusade for Christ, opened the joint session of the Florida state legislature with prayer. Within minutes after he prayed, a siege began against Dr. Bright, those who invited him, and public prayer. The state's newspapers announced in front-page articles that his invocation had offended others because he had made reference to the one true God in his prayers. This is the society in which we live. The tolerance of today is tolerant of everything except the truth.

Charles Colson says this about the church and culture:

> This is an historic moment of opportunity. When the church is faithful to its calling, it always leads to a reformation of culture. When the church is truly the church, a community living in biblical obedience and contending for faith in every area of life, it will surely revive the surrounding culture or create a new one.[4]

Your decision to open the Bible every day to look into the mirror and see truth from God makes you a light in a world filled with much darkness. Jesus said, "Let your light shine before men in such a way that they may see your good works, and glorify your Father who is in heaven" (Matthew 5:16). People who are committed to the truth will impact a culture. They will not just claim a life of love and joy but will be committed to it and carry it out in the place where they live. May you and I impact our culture because we live out the truth that we discover in God's Word.

My Response

DATE:

KEY VERSE: "Your word is truth" (John 17:17).

FOR FURTHER THOUGHT: What was your favorite insight about truth in today's reading? Did a new thought help you understand the importance of truth? Will you resolve to search out the truth in God's Word, knowing how relevant it is for your life? Think also about how your decisions about finding truth in the Bible will be a challenge to the culture of our day.

MY RESPONSE:

Day Nine

IT REALLY IS TRUE!

But whenever anyone turns to the
Lord, then the veil is taken away.

2 CORINTHIANS 3:16 NLT

No one can ignore evidence that confirms truth. When that evidence is overwhelming, it demands a verdict. Paul told the church at Corinth an amazing truth: "But whenever anyone turns to the Lord, then the veil is taken away" (2 Corinthians 3:16 NLT). There is an imperceptible moment when a person with many spiritual doubts about the Bible entertains a glimmer of hope: *What if it really is true?* This is the blessed beginning of a turn toward the Lord, and the veil that has blinded one's eyes to truth begins to disappear. That person experiences what the hymn writer said in "Amazing Grace": "I once was lost, but now am found, was blind, but now I see." The evidence of truth brings real sight and ultimately a change of life. Yesterday we saw the great value of truth in our lives. Today we want to see that there is evidence for the truth we have been given in the Bible.

I remember walking with my husband many years ago on a warm summer afternoon through the streets of Florence, Italy. We had toured many museums on our trip, and our fatigue had begun to catch up with us. So on this afternoon, we meandered along with no particular destination in mind. Our wandering brought us suddenly from an inconspicuous alley face-to-face with the doors of the Basilica di Santa Croce, the largest Franciscan church in Florence. We flipped through the pages of our guidebook, reinvigorated with energy at the treasure we had found. Once inside, we discovered murals by the famous Italian painter, Giotto di Bondone, considered to be the initiator of three-dimensional painting in Europe. Surrounding us were the tombs of no less famous people than Galileo and Michelangelo. Of course, I had read about these men of history in my history books, but to actually see their tombs confirmed the truth of their existence in history. And so it is with the Bible. I've heard people dismiss the existence of God and say that no one can prove the Bible. When I hear them say those things, I laugh. I believe more confirmation is available for the existence of God and the truthfulness of the Bible than for the events written in our history books.

Some of the most tangible evidence confirming the truth contained in the Word of God is in the area of archaeological finds. Howard F. Vos, in his book *Archaeology in Bible Lands,* says,

> Names of Gentile kings and the remains of numerous peoples thought to have been inventions of biblical scribes have come to light in the excavations. The historical validity of the patriarchal narrative has been reestablished, and at numerous other points the historicity of the Bible has been confirmed.[1]

Evidence of ancient cultures uncovered from the earth demonstrates the historicity of Scripture describing life in those cities. Geographical locations mentioned in the Bible are not mythological imaginings but real places where real people lived and worked. It is ancient history, not myth. Once you grasp that fact, your faith will grow and strengthen.

I have always loved archaeology. My introduction to this amazing field of study began one day in the Arizona desert where we camped with another family. We went motorcycle riding, and our adventures led us to explore some of the wilderness of the desert. I remember stopping my motorcycle because I noticed some pottery in the dirt by some rocks. I knelt down and saw some markings on the potsherd. As I brushed the dirt away, I found more pieces of pottery. When I returned home, I discovered that we were in an area known to have been inhabited by an ancient people group. Touching those pieces of pottery confirmed their existence to me and brought me closer to them in my own experience. When I became a Christian and began reading about events in the Bible, archaeology became more important to me. I was confident that archaeological finds were connected to real events in the Bible, thus confirming their occurrence in history. Little did I realize what was in store for me as I began my investigation.

Romance and excitement abound in the field of biblical archaeology. Each new discovery unearths an exciting story behind the archaeological find. The archaeologist, whether wielding a shovel or a small brush, unearths evidence of a distant culture. Some of the most exciting biblical archaeological finds include the buried city of Ugarit, the Ebla tablets, the Old Testament city of Edom, various New Testament finds, and the scrolls at Qumran.

In 1928, a farmer struck a large stone while plowing his field on the eastern coast of the Mediterranean Sea north of Beirut. Moving the stone out of the way, he discovered a passage leading to an ancient tomb filled with the possessions of the man buried there. Excavation of the area under that farmer's land uncovered the ancient town of Ugarit, a town that flourished just before the Exodus. Workers discovered tombs, houses, and hundreds of pottery bowls, jars, vases, tools, and weapons. In 1929, Claude Schaeffer, a French archaeologist, unearthed clay tablets with cuneiform writing that confirmed the existence of the land of Canaan spoken of in the Old Testament as the destination of the Exodus.

In 1964, Italian archaeologist Paolo Matthiae began excavations of Tell-Mardikh, a large mound covering 140 acres in northern Syria. By 1968, Matthiae had uncovered evidence of the lost city of Ebla. In 1974 and 1975, he excavated more than 20,000 tablets from the Ebla archives, the beginning of a spectacular ongoing archaeological enterprise. To date, the Ebla tablets have revealed a striking affinity with the language of Hebrew, the identification of patriarchal type names such as *abramu* (abram or abraham) and *israilu* (Israel), as well as the mention of geographical locations and names mentioned in the Bible including Hazor, Megiddo, Acco, Gaza, *Urusalima* (Jerusalem), Haran, and Ur.[2]

In 2 Samuel 8:13-14 (ESV) we learn that "David made a name for himself when he returned from striking down 18,000 Edomites in the Valley of Salt. Then he put garrisons in Edom; throughout all Edom he put garrisons, and all the Edomites became David's servants. And the LORD gave victory to David wherever he went." In December 2004, a team of scientists from Canada's McMaster University dated the nation of Edom to the exact time the Bible says it existed, that is, during the time of King David. The archaeological evidence affirms the existence of the Edomite people in the biblical period who were strong enough to fortify a city and establish a mining center.[3]

New Testament confirmation comes from numerous archaeological finds.

- John 18 speaks of Jesus facing a Roman governor named Pilate. In 1961, an Italian excavation uncovered an inscription at a Roman theater in Caesarea Maritima bearing the name "Pontius Pilate, prefect of Judea," the first physical evidence outside the Bible confirming his existence.

- John 5:2 says, "Now there is in Jerusalem by the sheep gate a pool, which is called in Hebrew Bethesda, having five porticoes." In 1956, archaeologists unearthed a rectangular pool with five porticoes in Bethesda, thus confirming the biblical account.

- John 19:13 describes the trial of Jesus at a place called "The Pavement...in Hebrew, Gabbatha." William F. Albright, in *The Archaeology of Palestine,* shows that this court was the court of the Antonia Fortress, the Roman military headquarters of Rome in Jerusalem. The court was destroyed between AD 66 and 70 during the siege of Jerusalem and left buried when the city was rebuilt in the time of Hadrian. In 1925, a French archaeologist named Vincent discovered a pavement stone bearing markings of an ancient game called The Game of the King. It is thought that is the game the Roman soldiers were playing when they were mocking Jesus at the Antonia Fortress. The inference is that this is the actual pavement of the judgment seat of the Roman governors, the place where Jesus stood as He was condemned to death by Pilate.

- John 19:18 describes the manner of Jesus' death: crucifixion. Despite many references to crucifixion in historical writings, no remains of a crucified victim had ever been found in Palestine. In 1968, the remains of a crucified man were found containing an ankle bone pierced with a seven-inch long nail. The iron was embedded in the bone and attached to a piece of olive wood from a cross. There was also evidence of the victim's leg bones having been broken.

In 1947, a shepherd, throwing rocks into caves in Qumran, northwest of the Dead Sea, heard the crack of breaking pottery, climbed up the cliff, and discovered earthen jars containing bundles of leather scrolls. Archaeologists invaded the region of about three hundred caves, yielding many additional scrolls and papyrus fragments, which we now call the Dead Sea Scrolls. Examination of these scrolls revealed many types of manuscripts—mostly biblical writings, but also commentaries on biblical books, apocryphal manuscripts, Old Testament pseudepigrapha, and sectarian literature.[4] Complete manuscripts, including a nearly complete scroll of Isaiah as well as tens of thousands of fragments of every book of the Hebrew Bible (except for Esther), established this as one of the greatest biblical archaeological finds of all time. What is the significance of such a find? The Dead Sea Scroll manuscripts are some of the oldest in existence today, bringing us closer than ever to the original biblical texts. They yield new information about life in Palestine from the second century BC to the first century AD, the development of the Bible, and the religious life in Palestine during the time of Christ. Overall, the Dead Sea Scrolls are an astounding discovery, bringing greater clarity to the setting of New Testament Christianity.

And the search continues for new discoveries. Who knows what other archaeological finds will confirm people and places we read about in the Bible? The more you explore the background of the Bible, the more material you have to draw upon as you read God's Word. This information grounds your faith and supports all you learn as you study God's Word. Such discoveries cause you to turn more and more to the Lord, which in turn gives you new sight and a view of the eternal.

My Response

DATE:

KEY VERSE: "But whenever anyone turns to the Lord, then the veil is taken away" (2 Corinthians 3:16 NLT).

FOR FURTHER THOUGHT: What is the value of archaeological discoveries to you as you study God's Word? What was your favorite archaeological discovery in today's reading?

MY RESPONSE:

THE HOLY SPIRIT
AND THE WORD

*The Helper, the Holy Spirit, whom the
Father will send in My name, He will
teach you all things, and bring to your
remembrance all that I said to you.*

JOHN 14:26

God speaks to you in His Word by His Holy Spirit. The Holy Spirit is vital for you to enjoy God's presence in His Word. Jesus said, "The Helper, the Holy Spirit, whom the Father will send in My name, He will teach you all things, and bring to your remembrance all that I said to you" (John 14:26). Jesus said to His disciples, "If anyone loves me he will keep my word; and my Father will love him, and We will come to him and make Our abode with him" (John 14:23). How does the Lord makes His home in us? It is through the Holy Spirit (see 2 Timothy 1:14). Paul says in 1 Corinthians 6:19 (AMP) that "your body is the temple (the very sanctuary) of the Holy Spirit Who lives within you." Our journey this week has shown us that the Bible is a mirror reflecting the truth. And now we want to understand how exactly we can see and understand the truth in the Bible.

I remember a special Christmas when my brother and I were still very young. It was the last Christmas that my grandfather was still with us. I suppose my mother and my grandfather had stayed up all night preparing for Christmas morning. When my brother and I leaped out of bed, sleepy-eyed, and ran into the hallway, we found the entrance to the living room completely hidden by a sheet hanging from the ceiling. We had to crawl through a tunnel created by the sheet until we made our way into the living room. The spectacle of the Christmas tree lights dazzled our eyes as we stood up to survey the entire living room floor covered with presents. Soon wrapping paper was flying into the air as we opened the presents one by one. Toys, books, a baseball bat and glove for my brother and, of course, a Barbie doll and her extensive wardrobe for me. But just as my brother and I had completed our mission with the presents, my grandfather told us we had to go on an errand. That was just about the last thing we wanted to do, but I'm glad we complied. At the end of the errand were two brand-new bicycles! I'll never forget that Christmas with my grandfather.

Can you imagine what would have happened that Christmas if we had not crawled through the tunnel to the presents? Can you imagine what would have happened if we had yawned and refused to go on that errand with my grandfather? We would have missed all the presents in the room and the new bicycles. Even so, many believers invite Jesus into their lives, but then they yawn and never understand the gift of the Holy Spirit, which the Lord gives to us at the moment of salvation.

All Christians are indwelt by the Holy Spirit (see John 14:15-17). A man named Nicodemus came to Jesus and asked if Jesus was from God. Jesus replied, "Unless one is born again he cannot see the kingdom of God…the wind blows where it wishes and you hear the sound of it…so is everyone who is born of the Spirit" (John 3:3-8). Romans 8:9 teaches that if you belong to God, the Spirit of God dwells in you."

The Holy Spirit is the third Person of the Trinity, the triune God. He has the nature of God, does the works of God, and has a specific function and purpose within the Godhead.

The Holy Spirit is a Person and has personality, meaning He possesses intellect, emotions, and will. He possesses the attributes and nature of God and is called the Spirit of God. If the Spirit is truly at work in your life, your life will be focused on Jesus Christ. The Holy Spirit is the One who gives you this experience of fellowship with Christ. You are the temple of the Holy Spirit. He is the one who keeps alive your fellowship with the Lord Jesus Christ.

The Holy Spirit and the Word of God

What is the relationship of the Holy Spirit to the Word of God? The Holy Spirit works hand in hand with the Word of God. He inspires it, illumines it, teaches it, and interprets it. He is the One who leads you into all truth (see John 16:13). Without the Holy Spirit, we could never know or love the Bible. James Montgomery Boice says "The Word without the illumination of the Holy Spirit remains a closed book."[1]

The Holy Spirit inspired the writing of the Word of God. Peter said, "But know this first of all, that no prophecy of Scripture is a matter of one's own interpretation, for no prophecy was ever made by an act of human will, but men moved by the Holy Spirit spoke from God" (2 Peter 1:20-21). Jesus, when quoting Psalm 110, pointed out that David spoke the words of the psalm "in the Holy Spirit" (Mark 12:36). Old Testament writers were aware that the Holy Spirit guided their writing (see 2 Samuel 23:2). Through the Holy Spirit, God wrote His love letter to you.

The Holy Spirit illumines the Word of God. When you read the Word of God, the Holy Spirit in you makes that Word come alive. When a verse is significant to you, the Holy Spirit has made it alive and outstanding to you. J. Hampton Keathley says illumination is "the special ministry of the Holy Spirit whereby He enlightens men so they can comprehend the written Word of God" (Ephesians 1:18; 3:9).[2] Paul said that no one can comprehend the thoughts of God except through the Holy Spirit (1 Corinthians 2:10-12). "Now we have received, not the spirit of the world, but the Spirit who is from God, so that we may know the things freely given to us by God" (1 Corinthians 2:12). Charles Ryrie says, "The experience of illumination is not by 'direct revelation.' The canon is closed. The Spirit illumines the meaning of that closed canon, and He does so through study and meditation."[3] Without the Holy Spirit, the Bible would be just words on a page.

The Holy Spirit teaches the Word of God. Jesus said, "But the Helper, the Holy Spirit, whom the Father will send in My name, He will teach you all things, and bring to your remembrance all that I said to you" (John 14:26). Jesus, in referring to the work of the Holy Spirit, says, "The Spirit of truth will bring glory to Me, because he will take what I have to say and tell it to you" (John 16:14 NCV). No teacher can compare to the Holy Spirit.

The Holy Spirit interprets the Word of God. Paul said, "And we impart this in words not taught by human wisdom but taught by the Spirit, interpreting spiritual truths to those who are spiritual. The natural person does not accept the things of the Spirit of God, for they are folly to him, and he is not able to understand them because they are spiritually discerned" (1 Corinthians 2:13-14 ESV). The Holy Spirit is your guide, sitting beside you as you study the Word, applying it to your life and bringing you to Christlikeness.

I'm reminded of the story of a nine-year-old boy who grew tired of practicing the piano. To inspire her son, the boy's mother took him to a concert by a famous pianist. There the boy sat, fidgeting in his little tuxedo, waiting for the concert to begin, as his mother visited with her friends. His eyes were drawn to the gleaming Steinway concert grand on the stage. Yielding to the urge, the boy slipped down the aisle, sat at the piano, and began playing the only song he knew, "Chopsticks." The audience was aghast, the mother embarrassed beyond words. But the great concert pianist came onto the stage, reached around the boy, and improvised a beautiful melody to go along with "Chopsticks." He encouraged the boy, "Keep playing, don't stop, don't quit."

In the same way the skilled pianist came alongside the young boy, the Holy Spirit illumines, interprets, and teaches the Word of God to you when you faithfully open its pages. The Holy Spirit is at work playing a beautiful melody in and through you. You have an amazing God who desires intimate fellowship with you. He has given you everything you need to make it possible—His magnificent Word and His indwelling Spirit. Will you open the pages of the Bible and discover what God wants to say to you?

My Response

KEY VERSE: "The Helper, the Holy Spirit, whom the Father will send in My name, He will teach you all things, and bring to your remembrance all that I said to you" (John 14:26).

FOR FURTHER THOUGHT: Why is the Holy Spirit important in your life? How does the Holy Spirit help you when you study God's Word? What was your most significant insight as you read today?

MY RESPONSE:

Day Eleven

THE GROUND OF
YOUR HEART

*The seed cast on good earth is the
person who hears and takes in the
News, and then produces a harvest
beyond his wildest dreams.*

MATTHEW 13:23 MSG

T he nature of your heart determines your receptivity to the Word. Is it soft, porous ground, drinking in the sustenance of what God has to say to you in the Bible, growing with each raindrop of the Word? Or is it cold, hard pavement, shunning God's voice, rejecting His persistent entreaty? Jesus was so concerned about the condition of the heart that He often followed His messages with a small but profound exhortation: "He who has ears to hear, let him hear" (Matthew 11:15). The burning question for those who desire to know and love the Bible is whether our hearts are willing to hear what God has to say to us when we study His Word.

It is often said that ten people who read a passage of Scripture can come away with ten entirely different responses. Some may say that the passage is boring without some application to their lives. Others admit that the passage is interesting but refuse to go any further in self-analysis. And then, for some, the passage is emotionally profound and changes their lives. A few may even discover their life verse. So then, what makes the difference? The receptive nature of your heart. Jesus speaks in Matthew 13:8-11 of the one heart where the seed fell on fertile soil, paraphrased as "good earth" in The Message, where the harvest was beyond one's "wildest dreams."

From Jesus' explanation of the harvest story in subsequent verses, one thing is clear: Your heart needs the Word. In fact, the Word actually softens the heart and makes it able to bear fruit. The challenge for you is not to be in the Word more, but to have more of the Word in you. It is not what you do in the Word but what the Word does in you. We see a powerful truth about the Word in Isaiah 55:10-11:

> For as the rain and the snow come down from heaven,
> And do not return there without watering the earth
> And making it bear and sprout,
> And furnishing seed to the sower and bread to the eater;
> So will My word be which goes forth from My mouth;
> It will not return to Me empty,
> Without accomplishing what I desire,
> And without succeeding in the matter for which I sent it.

God is likening the Word to rain and snow. Think about how rain permeates the ground and soaks deep down. Then consider the different types of rain. I remember walking on the beach in Hawaii, enjoying the mist of an afternoon rain lasting only 15 minutes. I got a little wet, but the ground hardly experienced the benefit of the rain. Ireland experiences "soft rain," a long, gentle rain reaching deep down into the ground. Snow, however, falls on frozen ground, eventually melting and making its way deeper in the dirt, but taking longer. In the same way, some hearts are in a season of cold and winter, taking longer to melt under the warming action of the Word.

William Shannon, in his book *Seeking the Face of God,* describes the similar action of the Word in our lives:

We shall derive little benefit from a quick, cursory reading of Scripture that skims over the words and lets them remain on the surface of our lives instead of reaching down deeply into the soil of our hearts. What is important is that, through *repeated, continuous, unhurried* reading, we allow our whole persons to be saturated, filled to overflowing, with the Word of God. We do not even, initially, at least, have to react to it. Instead we should simply let the Word happen to us. Let it be the soft, gentle, ongoing rain that comes into our lives and by its power makes them fertile and fruitful.[1]

The Latin term *lectio divina* refers to the practice of reading the Bible prayerfully, conscious of the presence of God. *Lectio divina* has long been a priority in the monastic tradition. Monks devote several hours each day to prayerful reading of the Word in monasteries. Life, for most of us, however, is not in the monastery. We live in the hurried pace of freeways, microwaves, computers, and busy schedules. We face a challenge: How can the Bible have its maximum impact on our hearts?

SLOW DOWN

When you slow down, you will hear God speak His Word as you read the pages of the Bible. You will see Him with the eyes of your heart as you learn about His character and ways. This is not mystical but spiritual. Spiritual truths, those secrets given by God in His Word, are seen with the eyes of your heart and mind. Paul prays in Ephesians 1:18-19 "that the eyes of your heart may be enlightened, so that you will know what is the hope of His calling, what are the riches of the glory of His inheritance in the saints, and what is the surpassing greatness of His power toward us who believe." The Holy Spirit must enlighten the eyes of your heart. The Greek word translated *enlighten* is *pethostismenous* and means to illuminate and give light.[2] You will see what others cannot see when you slow down and read verse by verse, line by line, and word by word. Your intention, your goal, is to see the Lord and to learn from Him. When you slow down in this way, your relationship with God will become intimate and personal.

PUT YOURSELF IN THE EVENT

Use your mind and your imagination when you read God's Word. Stop and think, *What if I were there in the situation, in the event?* Imagine you are in the crowd and perhaps even one of the people involved in an event. For example, in the Sermon on the Mount in Matthew 5–7, imagine yourself as one of the 12 disciples. How would you have felt to hear Jesus say those words? What might have been going through your mind as He spoke? I can almost feel the gentle breeze in my face as I listen to Him say, "Do not be anxious about your life, what you will eat or what you will drink, nor about your body, what you will put on. Is not life more than food, and the body more than clothing? Look at the birds of the air: they neither sow nor reap nor gather into barns, and yet your heavenly Father feeds them. Are you not of more value than they?" (Matthew 6:25-26 ESV). Perhaps at that very moment, when I hear those words from Jesus, I look in the sky and watch as a bird flies from one tree to another, seemingly untouched by the worries of the world. You can imagine yourself as a man or woman in the crowd, or a child standing afar off, looking at Jesus. As you immerse yourself in the event, you will begin to see spiritual truth as you have never seen it before. You will sense the presence of the Lord.

Some events are not conducive to this exact kind of imagination, such as genealogies in Numbers or laws in Leviticus. However, you can still immerse yourself in the passage by asking questions: Why is this being said? Why is this included in the Bible? What is the purpose? You begin thinking about the Word of God as His Word to you. That is how the Word becomes alive and you begin to see the Lord in every passage.

INTERACT AS YOU READ THE WORD

Interact with the Word as you read it. Ask questions as you look at each word, phrase, and verse. These questions may be personal: What is this telling me to do? Talk with the Lord as you read His Word. Remember, He is the one who has given His Word, and it has come from Him. You are talking with Him as Moses did, "face to face, just as a man speaks to his friend" (Exodus 33:11). Ask Him what He means. For example, when you read Jesus' words "In the world you have tribulation, but take courage; I have overcome the world" (John 16:33), you might be prompted to pray for someone who is in need.

Think About the Word Day and Night

Giving thought to a verse in the Bible allows for the great secrets in God's Word to surface. God said to Joshua, "Study this Book of the Law continually. Meditate on it day and night so you may be sure to obey all that is written in it. Only then will you succeed" (Joshua 1:8 NLT). The psalmist said, "My eyes anticipate the night watches, that I may meditate on Your Word" (Psalm 119:148). What do you think about most of the day? What do you think about when you awaken in the night? The challenge from the Lord is to think about what He says instead of immersing yourself in the worries and responsibilities of the day. Sometimes if I can't sleep at night, I will lie in bed and think about one verse after another—almost like having a complete Bible study just from Scripture I've learned in my quiet time. More than once, I've had to slip out of bed to write an insight about Scripture in my notebook.

Memorize Scripture

Often, during your time in the Word of God, you will discover a life-changing verse. Write this verse on a 3 x 5 index card and carry it with you, reviewing it throughout the day. You will find that you can memorize the Word with very little effort on your part. You can use index cards in several ways during your quiet time. You can use them to memorize scripture, record principles to review throughout the day, write out key verses to use in your prayer time, and keep a list of things to do that come to your mind during your quiet time. Try keeping some index cards in your *Quiet Time Notebook.*

The Great Result

Jesus said that when His Word is sown on the good soil of your heart, you will bear fruit. Fruit is the product of what is planted in your life. This spiritual fruit includes…

- reflecting the character of Christ—His love, joy, peace,

patience, kindness, goodness, faithfulness, gentleness, and self-control (Galatians 5:22-23)

• living a life worthy of the Lord (Colossians 1:10)

• leading others to Christ as a result of your life in Him (1 Peter 2:12)

When the Word of God is at work in your life, the outward evidence will be apparent for all to see. The spiritual fruit from the Word of God lasts forever. That means you can have a life that counts for eternity. It means that nothing you do is fleeting but substantial, important, and relevant to what God is doing in the world.

As we near the end of our second week, think about this question: How is your heart these days? Is your heart soft and able to receive the Word and go deep with God, or is it shallow, hard, and dry because of neglect of the Bible? Remember, yesterday's food cannot feed today's heart and soul. You need the words from God in the Bible every day in order to become more intimate with Him.

A young student came to his rabbi and asked him what he needed to do to become a teacher of the Scriptures himself. The rabbi asked him, "What have you done so far?" The student responded, "I have gone through the Torah." The rabbi then said, "Good, but has the Torah gone through you?" And so it is with you. One of the greatest secrets to knowing and loving the Bible is to be in the Word of God in such a way that it is soaking into you, permeating your heart, your soul, your entire being. May we sacrifice many good activities to realize this blessed eternal gift that God is offering to us in His Word.

My Response

DATE:

KEY VERSE: "The seed cast on good earth is the person who hears and takes in the News, and then produces a harvest beyond his wildest dreams" (Matthew 13:23 MSG).

FOR FURTHER THOUGHT: What do you learn from the picture of God's Word as rain or snow falling on your heart? Describe how the Bible makes a difference in your heart. How will this change your approach to the Word of God?

MY RESPONSE:

Day Twelve

QUIET TIME—
WEEK TWO:
EMBRACING THE
ROMANCE

PREPARE YOUR HEART

A young shoe salesman approached the superintendent of the Plymouth Congregational Church in the mid 1800s with a great desire on his heart—he wanted to teach Sunday school. The superintendent replied that he was sorry, but he already had enough Sunday school teachers. The young man protested that he did not desire to wait but wanted to begin right away. The superintendent suggested that he could start a small group and teach them in the countryside, and if they stayed together, he could bring them to church. The young man gathered the group together, took them to the beach at Lake Michigan, taught them Bible verses and Bible games, and took them to church. His name was Dwight Lyman Moody, and that was the beginning of a 40-year ministry reaching more than a hundred million people during his lifetime. One of the great secrets of D.L. Moody's life and ministry was his intense love for the Word of God. Moody said, "I never saw a useful Christian who was not a student of the Bible. If a man neglects his Bible, he may pray and ask God to use him in His work, but God cannot make much use of him; for there is not much for the Holy Spirit to work upon. We must have the Word itself, which is sharper than any two-edged sword."

As you begin this time with the Lord, how is your love for His Word? Do you open the pages of the Bible and stay there long enough to hear what God has to say? Begin by writing a prayer to the Lord, expressing all that is on your heart.

READ AND STUDY GOD'S WORD

Psalm 119 is one of the great passages about the Word of God. It offers so much to discover. One of the highlights is the psalmist's feelings about God's Word. Look at the following verses and record how the psalmist feels about the Word and what he does with the Word. You may want to underline the most significant phrases in your Bible.

verses 11-16

verse 20

verse 31

verses 47-48

verse 81

verse 93

verse 97

verse 103

verse 111

Summarize what you have learned from Psalm 119.

ADORE GOD IN PRAYER

Psalm 119 is a prayer directed to God Himself. Will you pray Psalm 119:33-40 to the Lord today?

YIELD YOURSELF TO GOD

There are times when solitude is better than society, and silence is wiser than speech. We should be better Christians if we were more alone, waiting upon God, and gathering through meditation on His Word spiritual strength for labour in His service...Our souls are not nourished merely by listening awhile to this, and then to that, and then to the other part of divine truth. Hearing, reading, marking, and learning, all require inwardly digesting to complete their usefulness, and the inward digesting of the truth lies for the most part in meditating upon it.

CHARLES HADDON SPURGEON
Morning and Evening

ENJOY HIS PRESENCE

As you think about D.L. Moody and the writer of Psalm 119 and their love for God's Word, what have you learned that will help you grow in your own love for the Word of God? Close your time in God's Word by talking with the Lord about your own desire to know and live out His Word.

REST IN HIS LOVE

"Remember the word to Your servant, in which You have made me hope. This is my comfort in my affliction, that Your word has revived me" (Psalm 119:49-50).

Notes—Week Two

Week Three

EXPLORE THE
ROMANCE

Days 13-18

JOURNEY THROUGH THE BIBLE

*Let the word of Christ richly
dwell within you.*

COLOSSIANS 3:16

Your journey in God's Word is the true measure of your spiritual wealth. A journey implies a starting point, discovery along the way, and a destination. A Bible reading plan will help you on your journey. Paul encourages us to "let the word of Christ richly dwell" in us. That means we are to be extravagant with the Bible, seeking a rich, spiritual journey rather than accepting a dry, academic exercise. I have used many exciting Bible reading plans, including Bible studies, devotional Bibles, and reading through the Bible in a year. I challenge you to consider reading through the Bible in a year.

During the last two weeks, we have explored the great value of the Bible; its beauty, depth, and power. We want to know it and love it. Spending time in the Bible will yield amazing results. But what does that look like in everyday life? You're busy. I'm busy. We've got computers, carpools, e-mail, jobs, family, and countless responsibilities. How could we possibly consider reading through the entire Bible in a year? Perhaps the better question is how can we make reading through the Bible in a year a rich, spiritual journey? The quality of our devotional Bible study will be the focus of the remainder of this book. But first we must make a commitment, and then we will enjoy the devotional response. Our commitment to a Bible reading plan such as reading through the Bible in a year is the first step. This is your opportunity.

My friend and fellow author Jim Smoke serves with me in the adult ministries department at our church. We were talking one day about devotional Bible study, as we often do, and we decided to issue a challenge to our ministries, both women and seniors, to read through the Bible in a year. We chose *The Daily Walk Bible* in the New Living Translation. We ordered 200 Bibles and challenged our groups to read through the Bible. We sold out of those Bibles in a week. Many people in the women's and seniors' ministries became so excited that they purchased one for each member of their family. The senior pastor took the idea to the pulpit and announced it in our church service. We sold out of another 200 Bibles almost immediately. A woman attending that church service bought some of the Bibles, returned home to Seattle, Washington, and began passing them out as gifts to pastors in the Northwest. Suddenly, what had begun in two small groups in a local church had spread to thousands throughout the western United States, and all in just a few weeks. The publisher sold out of the Bibles and had to publish more.

We began our journey through the Bible with an air of excitement and discovery. Many people told me they were reading through the Bible with their spouses, their children, and other family members for the very first time. We created a website at www.OnlineReadingGroup.com that was coordinated with our Bible reading plan and that included devotionals written by both Jim Smoke and me. The result was that many were reading God's love letter to them in its entirety instead of in bits and pieces. The Bible suddenly made sense to them. The yearly devotional Bible had given each person a daily Bible reading plan. Some became consistent in their quiet time for the first time. For those who were new to the Bible, their experience helped familiarize them with how the Bible is organized from Genesis to Revelation. This is just the start of the fantastic journey of devotional Bible study. Now it's your turn.

HOW TO JOURNEY THROUGH THE BIBLE IN A YEAR

How can you read through the Bible in a year? First, choose a one-year devotional Bible that uses your favorite translation and is organized in a way that makes sense to you.

- *The Daily Walk Bible* (NLT or NIV, Tyndale House Publishers)—includes devotional introductions.

- *The Daily Bible* (NIV, Harvest House Publishers, by F. LaGard Smith)—one of my favorites, organized in a historical, chronological format with insightful devotional commentary.

- *The One Year Bible* (KJV, NASB, NLT, NIV, ESV, Tyndale House Publishers)—each daily reading includes passages from the Old Testament, the New Testament, Psalms, and Proverbs without other devotional material.

- *The NIV Men's or Women's Devotional Bible* (NIV, Zondervan)—includes devotional readings and a one-year reading plan.

Second, determine when to begin your journey. Although the most common time to begin is January 1, there's no time like the present. If you begin tomorrow, turn to that date and start at that point. Don't try to read hundreds of pages just to catch up. If you miss a day, continue with the next day.

Third, use a notebook or journal to record your insights each day. You will be amazed at what you notice along the way. This year I've been reading through *The Daily Walk Bible*. Here's what I wrote in my journal one day about the life of Joseph from Genesis 41:

> From the life of Joseph I see how God prepares a person to accomplish His purposes. Joseph was in prison for many years. And yet in that dark place, through extreme measures, Joseph learned the skills to lead a nation. The dark place,

the trouble, the suffering, can be the training ground for God's plans and purposes in my life and can influence my generation. Look how Joseph's exaltation by God is seen in the names of his two sons, Manasseh and Ephraim, describing what God did for Joseph. Manasseh means *"God has made me forget all my troubles and the family of my father,"* and Ephraim means *"God has made me fruitful in the land of my suffering."* I'm encouraged to know that regardless of how dark the day, it is always too soon to give up. Fruitfulness is just around the corner.

Face-to-Face with God in the Bible

Keep in mind the following guidelines as you draw near to God in His Word:

Read with the goal to know and love God. Moses said, "If you are pleased with me, teach me your ways so I may know you and continue to find favor with you" (Exodus 33:13 NIV). Always be listening for God's voice in His Word, remembering that God is speaking by the Holy Spirit and articulating truth for you. Do not go outside of God's Word to hear God's voice.

Read with a heart for God and a teachable spirit. David said, "You are my God. I worship you. In my heart, I long for you, as I would long for a stream in a scorching desert" (Psalm 63:1 CEV). The psalmist says, "Open my eyes, that I may behold wonderful things from Your law" (Psalm 119:18). You don't have to be an intellectual or have academic diplomas to know and love the Bible. You simply must desire to have a heart-to-heart relationship with the Lord, to learn from Him, and to hear Him speak.

Read with an expectation of thrill and delight. "I shall delight in Your statutes; I shall not forget Your word" (Psalm 119:16). Contained within God's Word are sights that you could never imagine, even in your wildest dreams. As you read God's Word under the tutelage of the Holy Spirit, it will become life to you. The Lord will apply His Word to your heart and transform you into someone you never thought you could be.

Read with an understanding of God's plan. "God so loved the world, that He gave His only begotten Son, that whoever believes in Him shall not perish, but have eternal life. For God did not send the Son into the world to judge the world, but that the world might be saved through Him" (John 3:16-17). The Bible unfolds God's plan from Genesis to Revelation. History really is "His story," the true story of how God has rescued you so you can spend eternity with Him. The Old Testament points forward to Jesus, and the New Testament reveals Jesus. The Bible provides everything you need in order to know God and understand His plan. It reveals a story of love, redemption, salvation, and glory. Beginning in Genesis 3:15 you will discover more than 300 prophecies pointing to a Messiah who would save His people from their sins. This Messiah would be born through the nation of Israel. God established a relationship with the people of Israel to be their God. His desire was that they would belong to Him. Through many different prophets, God laid out a map of who the Messiah would be, what He would be like, what He would do, and why He would do it. Jesus was born at just the right time, in the line of David. And Jesus claimed to be God. He was crucified on a cross, not for what He did but for who He claimed to be.

Read with a knowledge of an overview of the entire Bible. "You search the Scriptures because you think that in them you have eternal life; it is these that testify about Me" (John 5:39). The Bible reveals this plan of God's redemption for you and me through Jesus. The historical books of the Bible chronicle the history of Israel, God's people. These books include Genesis, Exodus, Leviticus, Numbers, Deuteronomy, Joshua, Judges, Ruth, 1 and 2 Samuel, 1 and 2 Kings, 1 and 2 Chronicles, Ezra, Nehemiah, and Esther. In these books you can learn who God is and how He relates to His people. The Law displays the perfection of His standard and your own need for a Savior. The covenants (solemn, binding agreements) between God and His people demonstrate the importance of your relationship with God through Jesus. The poetic books of the Bible are Job, Psalms, Proverbs, Ecclesiastes, and the Song of Solomon. These books contain the worship, prayers, and wisdom of the people of Israel—especially the Psalms. They provide great insight as you draw near to your Lord and worship Him. The 17 prophetic books of the Old Testament include Isaiah, Jeremiah, Lamentations, Ezekiel, Daniel, Hosea, Joel, Amos, Obadiah, Jonah, Micah, Nahum,

Habakkuk, Zephaniah, Haggai, Zechariah, and Malachi. The primary function of the prophets was to speak for God to their contemporaries about His character and His covenant. You might think of the prophecies about the future as God revealing His secrets and plans to His people before these events actually take place. Some prophecies pertain to the first coming of Jesus as the Suffering Servant and some to His second coming as the Conquering King.

The New Testament begins with the four Gospels: Matthew, Mark, Luke, and John. Each of these four books reveals specific details of Jesus' life and character. Then, Acts reveals the formation of the early church and its ministry following the death, burial, and resurrection of Jesus. It displays the nature and purpose of the church and Jesus' continuing ministry of touching hearts and changing lives in and through the church. The New Testament also contains 21 letters written by Paul, John, Peter, James, Jude, and the writer of Hebrews. These letters present countless truths about how to live the Christian life and walk with the Lord. Finally, the Bible tells the rest of God's story in Revelation and ends with a picture of eternal life with Christ in heaven.

Read with the knowledge that the Bible contains everything you need to know about the redemption story. "His divine power has granted to us everything pertaining to life and godliness, through the true knowledge of Him who called us by His own glory and excellence" (2 Peter 1:3). The Bible contains what God has chosen to reveal to you in order to live and walk and grow and thrive with Him. It is His gift to you. You can choose to make the most of what He has given to you. "The secret things belong to the LORD our God, but the things revealed belong to us and to our sons forever, that we may observe all the words of this law" (Deuteronomy 29:29).

YOUR BIBLE READING PLAN AND YOUR QUIET TIME

You can incorporate a one-year Bible reading plan into the P.R.A.Y.E.R. Quiet Time Plan (see *Six Secrets to a Powerful Quiet Time*, Harvest House Publishers). As you begin your quiet time, you might take a few moments to Prepare Your Heart with a psalm or a devotional reading from a book like *My Utmost for His Highest* by Oswald Chambers. Then Read and Study God's Word by reading in your one-year Bible (or using another Bible reading plan) and digging a little deeper with devotional Bible study (which we will learn about in the next few days). Then Adore God in Prayer by talking with God about what you have read. Then Yield Yourself to God by thinking for a few moments about what you have learned in your Bible reading. How can you apply what you have learned to your life? You might write a prayer to the Lord in your journal expressing all that is on your heart. Then Enjoy His Presence by carrying what you have learned in your quiet time with you throughout the day. And Rest in His Love with the peace and confidence that you have met with the Lord, you are never alone, and He is with you to guide and strengthen you all along the way. Your quiet time with God is the place where you daily meet with Him. The P.R.A.Y.E.R. Quiet Time Plan will help you get the most out of your time alone with the Lord whether you have 15 minutes or an hour.

Reading through the Bible in a year will help you stay in the Bible every day, and you can choose a new one-year Bible each year. Find some friends to share in your Bible reading adventure. Get together once a week to share what you are learning. Reading about 15 minutes a day will probably take you through the Bible in a year. Those could be the most important 15 minutes of your day. And, my friend, this is only the beginning. Get ready for the journey.

My Response

DATE:

KEY VERSE: "Let the word of Christ richly dwell within you" (Colossians 3:16).

FOR FURTHER THOUGHT: Have you ever read through the Bible in a year? If so, what did you learn from your experience? Will you make a commitment to take the journey through the Bible? If so, which Bible are you going to choose for this year?

MY RESPONSE:

Day Fourteen

DISCOVERING SECRETS IN THE WORD

*I will show you secrets you
have never known.*

ISAIAH 48:6 CEV

God wants to tell you His secrets. He says, "Pray to me and I will answer you. I will tell you important secrets you have never heard before" (Jeremiah 33:3 NCV). We learn from the psalmist in Psalm 25:14 (TLB), "Friendship with God is reserved for those who reverence Him. With them alone He shares the secrets of His promises." When you know people's secrets, they include you in their inner circle. God's inner circle is called "friendship with God." God says, "I will show you secrets you have never known" (Isaiah 48:6 CEV). These truths that God wants to show His people remain hidden if we neglect what He says in His Word. Most people are observers rather than participants with God. Many feel as though a great distance separates them from God. When one reads the Bible as unfamiliar territory without any knowledge of how to traverse it, this sense of distance grows. Wouldn't you rather be a friend of God than a stranger? Wouldn't you love to have Him tell you His secrets?

When my husband and I first moved to Palm Desert, California, I felt alone and disconnected from everything I knew and loved. I would drive down unfamiliar roads, take wrong turns, and end up in the strangest places. After a year of driving around the area, everything had become so familiar that I began to enjoy the beauty of my new desert surroundings. I found favorite stores, restaurants, and wonderful friends that added to that sense of familiarity. It became my home.

What will help you come to the place where the Bible becomes familiar territory with countless roads that take you straight to the heart of God? What will make the Bible a home to you? What will help you hear and see God's secrets in His Word? Adding devotional Bible study to your quiet time. What this will mean for you, practically speaking, is that you will sit with the Bible for a few extra moments in your quiet time and think more deeply about what it says as you are reading. It means you will take a little extra time to explore the meaning of what you are reading and write out your insights in your journal or notebook.

Early in my relationship with God I became confused about what to do with the Bible. I knew I should spend quiet time with God. I knew that reading the Bible was a part of that quiet time. Then I heard people talk about Bible study. I wondered, *When am I supposed to do that? In my quiet time? Or at another time?* Perhaps you have had these same questions. Over the years I have learned how to incorporate devotional Bible study into my quiet time. The Greek word translated *devote* is *prokarteo* and means to tarry, remain somewhere, or remain long with the thought. In devotional Bible study, we want to tarry awhile in the Word of God in our quiet time. I love Merrill C. Tenney's definition of devotional Bible study:

> Devotional study impresses the message on a believing heart. The crown of all study is devotional study. Devotional study is not so much of a technique as a spirit. It is the spirit of eagerness which seeks the mind of God; it is the spirit of humility which listens readily to the voice of God; it is

the spirit of adventure which pursues earnestly the will of God; it is the spirit of adoration which rests in the presence of God.[1]

Early on, I noticed that Amy Carmichael, in her devotional book *The Edges of His Ways,* shared many insights from the Bible: a new observation, a special insight on a verse, application of the verse to an experience, a different translation of a verse, the definition of a word in a verse, or several verses related to a topic. I realized that what she shared was a result of her devotional quiet time in the Word. I thought to myself, *Why can't I incorporate these devotional studies into my quiet time as well?* And so I decided to become creative as I sat with God in His Word. Learning principles of biblical interpretation in seminary has also added new ideas for devotional Bible study in my quiet time.

Devotional Bible study means taking time in your Bible reading to tarry awhile to discover God's secrets and meet Him face-to-face. When you read your passage of Scripture in your quiet time, you will notice a significant word, phrase, person, or verse. Take some time to look for one of the following opportunities to dig deeper when you read and study God's Word:

- *Observation study.* Do you notice a group of interesting facts about a topic such as faith in Hebrews 11, or a person, such as Jesus in John 1? You can make a list of what you notice. You will be amazed at the profound insight that can come from looking more closely at a passage of Scripture and writing out what you see.

- *Translation study.* Is a particular verse meaningful to you in your quiet time? You can look it up in another translation. Sometimes another translation helps you see something new and profound in a verse that you never saw before.

- *Reference or topical study.* Is a certain phrase in a verse or topic significant to you in your quiet time? You can look at other verses in the Bible that relate to your chosen phrase or topic. Looking at other verses helps reveal the meaning of the Word of God.

- *Verse study.* Does a verse contain words you would like to understand better? You can look up the meanings of all those words in exciting word study tools.

- *Word study.* Does your Bible reading include one word that you would like to define? You can look up its meaning in several word study dictionaries.

- *Character study.* Would you like to know more about a biblical character in your Bible reading? You can take time to study people's lives and record insights that will apply to your own life.

- *Doctrine or ethics study.* Would you like to become more clear about what you believe? You can collect verses related to a particular subject.

In devotional Bible study, you read the Bible, write out what you are learning, and allow God's Word to make its way into the deepest places of your heart. Devotional Bible study is not something you will necessarily have time to do every day. You will not use all these techniques at once. But you want to go deeper on some days. These ways to dig deeper will help you do exactly that—go deeper for treasure in the Bible. Devotional study takes only an additional five to ten minutes of your quiet time. Or it can take longer, depending on how much time you have and how much time you are willing to give. Devotional study is not meant to take the place of inductive Bible study in a particular book of the Bible. It is meant to take you deeper in your Bible reading, day by day. It allows you to learn powerful truths from God. Devotional Bible study is what you can do any day of the week during your quiet time. And when you do, you will discover God's magnificent secrets.

DISCOVERING THE SECRETS

Here are just a few examples of the secrets of God I have discovered in His Word:

- *The secret of contentment.* "In any and every circumstance I have learned the secret of being filled and going hungry, both of having abundance and suffering need" (Philippians 4:12). I remember when I first discovered this verse; it helped me understand that contentment in life depends on my relationship with the Lord and not my outward circumstances.

- *The secret of weakness.* "'Power is perfected in weakness.' Most gladly, therefore, I will rather boast about my weaknesses, so that the power of Christ may dwell in me...for when I am weak, then I am strong" (2 Corinthians 12:9-10). When I discovered this verse, I learned that God can do great and mighty things in and through me even when I am weak.

- *The secret of the inner life.* "But when you pray, go into your room and shut the door and pray to your Father who is in secret. And your Father who sees in secret will reward you" (Matthew 6:6 ESV). This is a powerful secret because it demonstrates that my quiet time with God is important to Him.

- *The secret of faith.* "We walk by faith, not by sight" (2 Corinthians 5:7 ESV). This verse shows me the secret about how I am to live my life, taking God at His Word by faith.

- *The secret of the kingdom of God.* "To you it has been given to know the secrets of the kingdom of God" (Luke 8:10 ESV). This verse tells me that all of life is wrapped up in God's kingdom, not the things of this world.

- *The secret of the future.* "I will show you secrets you have never known" (Isaiah 48:6 ESV). This secret helps me understand that God knows the future, and He lets His children know what we need to know in advance. A great example is the book of Revelation, where God lets me know "the rest of the story."

God will reveal literally hundreds if not thousands of secrets to you when you draw near to Him in His Word. As Paul told the church at Corinth, "No mere man has ever seen, heard, or even imagined what wonderful things God has ready for those who love the Lord" (1 Corinthians 2:9 TLB).

My Response

DATE:

KEY VERSE: "I will show you secrets you have never known" (Isaiah 48:6 CEV).

FOR FURTHER THOUGHT: What is the value of knowing the secrets of God? What will it take to know His secrets? What did you learn today that helps you know how to dig deeper into the Bible?

MY RESPONSE:

Day Fifteen

ENGAGING IN THE ROMANCE

Be diligent to present yourself approved
to God, a worker who does not need to be
ashamed, rightly dividing the word of truth.

2 TIMOTHY 2:15 NKJV

When you fall in love with the Lord, you will study what He says to know Him in a deep and meaningful way. You can't help it. You love Him. This is devotional study of the Word of God, the practice of drawing near to God in His Word, the Bible. And God encourages your passion to know Him; He loves your embrace of this romance. He says through Paul in 2 Timothy 2:15 to "Be diligent to present yourself approved to God, a worker who does not need to be ashamed, rightly dividing the word of truth." When Paul taught the Word of God in Berea, the Bereans "received the word with great eagerness, examining the Scriptures daily to see whether these things were so. Therefore many of them believed" (Acts 17:11-12). Like the Bereans, you will do well to not merely read the Word of God but study it with eagerness. As you search and examine the Word, you will learn what is true. Regard the Bible the way you would a long-awaited letter from the one you love the most—as a treasure.

THE ADVENTURE OF DEVOTIONAL BIBLE STUDY

When you think of adventure, you might think of the movie hero Indiana Jones trekking through the jungle, searching for an archaeological dig, eager to find a wealth of treasure. But for me, from an early age, adventure has been synonymous with the NASA space missions to the final frontier. I will never forget sitting cross-legged in front of a small black-and-white television, watching with my mother as Alan Shepard became the first American in space, maneuvering the *Freedom 7* space capsule. Breathtaking. And then, years later, on a hot, summer July day, I sat mesmerized, watching Neil Armstrong and Buzz Aldrin walk on the moon. Inspiring. But how much greater is the adventure of studying the Word of God. I often meditate on 1 Corinthians 2:9-10 in relation to studying God's Word: "...things which eye has not seen and ear has not heard, and which have not entered the heart of man, all that God has prepared for those who love Him. For to us God revealed them through the Spirit." The Greek word for *study, spoudazo,* implies eagerness. The Lord is taking you on an exciting adventure designed just for you. When you take time to look more closely at what God is saying in the Bible, you are in for the adventure of your life.

LIVING THE ADVENTURE OF DEVOTIONAL BIBLE STUDY

Write down what it says. Writing your thoughts and observations causes your mind to think in new directions, considering each thought with a deeper intensity, expanding your love and appreciation for the Bible. At first as you are writing, you may think, *Where did that thought come from!* It is always an exciting moment when the Lord teaches you from His Word. I'll never forget the morning I read Genesis 8:1, "But God remembered Noah." Those four words caught my attention. I opened my notebook and began writing. The word *remembered* was especially significant to me. From a previous quiet time study I knew the Hebrew word for *remembered* meant that God paid special attention to

Noah and lavished care and concern on him. As I wrote, I looked at the next verse and noticed that God sent a wind to blow across the waters. As I wrote out that verse in my notebook, I had a new thought: *In an imperceptible moment, God sends something our way to change the face of our circumstances just as He did when He sent the wind to blow across the waters.* Then I wrote out the next part of the verse: "The floods began to disappear." God does change our circumstances in His way and in His time. As He remembered Noah, so He remembers me. It was a powerful time with the Lord, my Bible, and my *Quiet Time Notebook.*

Personalize what you see. You can write in a literal way or a personal way. I have found that personalizing what I see will bring to light many secrets in God's Word for me. For example, in John 6:35, the literal observation is that He who comes to Jesus will not hunger, and he who believes in Jesus will never thirst. The more *personal* observation is that if I come to Jesus, I will not hunger, and if I believe in Jesus, I will never thirst. Which way means more to you? When I change the impersonal *he* to the personal *I,* the truths become real to me. God is the God of the individual, the one He has created for a relationship with Him. He is interested in speaking to you and transforming your heart. Personalizing what you see in God's Word helps you realize its relevance. It is not only something that was written thousands of years ago for other people. No, it is also God's Word for you today where you live.

Meditate on God's Word. Taking time with God's Word is essential; engaging in Christian meditation of God's Word is life-changing. Christian meditation is biblical. J.I. Packer points out that Christian meditation is an activity of holy thought; it dwells on the works, ways, purposes, and promises of God; and it is accomplished with the help of God. It is communion with God, and it impacts one's mind and heart.[1] Carry what you have learned in your devotional study by meditating on a significant verse throughout the day.

YOUR APPROACH: READ AND STUDY GOD'S WORD

The Read and Study God's Word format in the P.R.A.Y.E.R. Quiet Time Plan and included in the *Quiet Time Notebook* is a way to devotionally study any passage of Scripture in the Bible. See figure 1 on page 132. This format leads you to ask three questions: What does it say, what does it mean, and what does it mean to me? These are frequently referred to as observation, interpretation, and application. Observation helps you see everything in a passage. Interpretation determines what it means, taking into account rules of interpretation such as context, type of language, type of literature, author, and background. Application applies what you have learned to your own life.

In the days to come you will learn seven exciting ways to devotionally study the Bible. But first, let's review the steps to Read and Study God's Word:

Read God's Word and record one significant observation. I write in my journal or notebook a word, a verse, or a phrase that seems most significant to me. For example, in James 1:1-3 my significant observation would be that the testing of my faith produces endurance.

Note the immediate context. I look at the surrounding verses in the passage of Scripture and note how my one significant observation relates to them. For example, in James 1:1-3, the testing of my faith is referred to in a passage all about trials. Please remember that immediate context depends on the general context of any passage. Many Bible students make the mistake of reading their own time, place, and culture into the passage in an attempt to make an immediate application to their lives. Context rules in the interpretation of any passage of Scripture. Questions always lead to discovery. Every time you study Scripture, certain facts are important:

- *Historical background.* Who wrote it? Note the author and occasion.

- *Cultural background.* When was it written? Describe the cultural setting.

- *Geographical content.* Where was it written? Record the location, distances, topography.

- *Type of literature and language.* What is written? Determine whether the passage contains poetry, correspondence, prophecy, history, an apocalypse, a narrative, wisdom sayings, or gospel stories. Is it figurative language?

- *Immediate content.* How is it written? Summarize the passage as a whole.

- *Theme and purpose.* Why was it written? Identify the main idea and objective.

One of the easiest ways to discover the answers to these questions of context is to look up the book of the Bible you are studying in a Bible dictionary or encyclopedia. For example, if you were to look up Philippians in the *New Bible Dictionary* you would learn that it is a letter written by Paul to the Philippian church while he was in prison. I also use the notes at the beginnings of each book in my *NIV Study Bible* to discover context. *Halley's Bible Handbook* by Henry H. Halley or *What the Bible Is All About* by Henrietta Mears are two other great tools to help you understand context as you are reading through the Bible. A wonderful tool to discover context for yourself is *Discover the Bible for Yourself* by Kay Arthur.

Insights, word meanings, and cross-references. I go deeper with my one significant observation: I (1) write out my insights, (2) look up the meaning of a word, or (3) cross-reference the verse using my cross-reference Bible or *The Treasury of Scripture Knowledge.* For example, in James 1:1-3 we see that trials can be productive. The Greek word for *endurance* (*Strong's* #5281—*hupomone*) refers to the "quality that does not surrender under circumstances or succumb under trial." I learn from the cross-reference 1 Peter 1:6-7 that the proof of my faith is more precious than gold and will result in praise and glory at the revelation of Christ. Please remember to determine the original, intended meaning of the passage of Scripture. This is often called grammatico-historical interpretation.[2] God included each part of the Bible, His Word, to teach specific principles of spiritual truth. He intends for you to discover one meaning, but different applications will surface as God speaks to each of us in our own life circumstances.

Summary and conclusions. I write out two or three sentences summarizing what I have learned. This helps me articulate what is most important to me from my time in God's Word. For example in James 1:1-3 I note that I can have joy in trials and that a trial makes me stronger so that I won't surrender to adverse circumstances.

Application in my life. I ask the Lord, *What do you want to teach me today from what I have learned? How can this change my life?* Then I write in my journal or notebook what the Lord has impressed on my heart. For example, in James 1:1-3 I write about strength to stand strong in the current trial, and I write a prayer to the Lord for His perspective. Charles Ryrie emphasizes the importance of application: "Study employs all the proper tools for ascertaining the meaning of the text. Meditation thinks about the true facts of the text, putting them together into a harmonious whole and applying them to one's own life." God does not give His Word to you for academic exercise. He intends for it to change your life. When you read and study God's Word, you might ask yourself some probing questions to help you apply what you have learned in your own life:

- How does what you have learned give you God's view of your present situation in life?

- What do you learn about God and His ways?

- Does God want you to obey something?

- Have you been convicted of a sin requiring confession and repentance?

- How has God met your needs and present circumstances in life today?

- Did you find an example from which you can pattern your own life?

- Does a doctrinal or ethical truth command your belief and require a change in your behavior?

- Did you learn anything that affects your goals in life, giving you new meaning and purpose?

- Can you encourage someone with a letter, book, or phone call?

- Do you know someone who needs an expression of God's love, the message of the gospel, or a need met today?

ENGAGING IN THE ROMANCE

Variety, spontaneity, and consistency are essential in your relationship with God. These qualities need not be mutually exclusive. Some mornings you may choose to dig deeper in your quiet time with one of the devotional studies you will learn in this book.

Keep in mind that you are not going to do these studies all at once or every day. In fact, you will often have time for only Bible reading and perhaps writing a verse or an insight in your journal. Some studies will become your favorites and will yield a treasure if you are willing to pay the price in time and energy to draw near to God in His Word. Remember that devotional Bible study is something that is learned and practiced—and it's fun! Take some time to learn, and get ready for an incredible adventure.

Are you thirsty to know God in a deeper way? Do you have a passion to love Him and become all He wants you to be? Do you long for those rivers of living water that Jesus talked about for those who believe in Him? A.W. Tozer pointed out that those who find God in a way that others do not are the ones who cultivate the lifelong habit of spiritual response. Nowhere is this more true than in your romance with God and His Word. When you respond to God as He leads you in His Word, your life with Him will move from a journey to an adventure and a romance. Are you willing to stop long enough to listen as the Lord speaks to you? Will you sit at His feet and hear His Word? Will you turn from the distractions of the world and open your heart toward the Lord? Always remember that the Holy Spirit is your teacher. As you engage in the romance of studying God's Word, always begin with prayer, asking God to speak to you and to give you a listening heart.

Read and Study God's Word

"Study this book of the Law continually.
Meditate on it day and night" (Joshua 1:8 NLT).

Date: _Jan 21, 2005_____ Today's Scripture: _James 1:1-3_____

Read God's Word and record one significant observation:

The testing of my faith produces endurance.

Immediate context:

This passage is all about trials.

Insights / word meanings / cross-references:

Insight: trials can be productive.

Endurance—5281—hupomone—the quality that does not surrender under circumstances or succumb under trial

1 Peter 1:6-7—The proof of my faith is more precious than gold and will result in praise and glory at the revelation of Christ.

Summary and conclusions:

It is possible to have joy in trials. A trial makes me stronger so that I won't surrender to adverse circumstances.

Application in my life:

This gives me the strength to stand strong in the current trial. Lord, help me see your perspective in the difficult circumstances of life.

FIGURE 1: READ AND STUDY GOD'S WORD PAGE
FROM THE *QUIET TIME NOTEBOOK*

My Response

DATE:

KEY VERSE: "Be diligent to present yourself approved to God as a workman who does not need to be ashamed, accurately handling the word of truth" (2 Timothy 2:15).

FOR FURTHER THOUGHT: What have you learned about devotional Bible study today? What is the most important insight you gained from your reading? What value do you think devotional Bible study will add to your quiet time? Was there a new idea that will help you as you spend time with God in His Word?

MY RESPONSE:

SURPRISED BY THE BIBLE

*Angels would have given
anything to be in on this!*

1 PETER 1:12 MSG

Every day is a new day when you open the pages of your Bible. God wants to show you things you have never seen before. And He often uses your quiet time as the catalyst for surprise. Peter points out that the Holy Spirit reveals truth to us that is so amazing that "even the angels are eagerly watching these things happen" (1 Peter 1:12 NLT). The more you look in the mirror of God's Word, the more you will see. And the more you see, the more you will know your Lord. The more you know Him, the more you will love Him. And the more you love Him, the more you will fall on your knees in worship of Him. The secret is learning new ways to look in the mirror of God's Word.

From our table in a villa restaurant in the hillside town of Fiesole, my husband and I took in our first expansive view of the Arno Valley, which encompasses the renaissance city of Florence, Italy. At first our eyes only accepted the verdant green landscape of this glorious, sunny afternoon. Then each of the red-tiled domes peeked out from the valley floor as the cathedrals and churches caught our attention. A few more minutes passed before we noticed the fragrance of jasmine from the hillside floral display. As we sat there we soon appreciated the distant sound of the bells tolling from the Duomo, Florence's largest cathedral. Before long, our senses exploded with the symphony of beauty in this scenic valley. The longer we sat, the more we saw.

And so it is in your quiet time. The more you observe, the more you will see. Often you will want to think about a particular passage in a deeper way. You can do an observation study, simply writing down everything you notice in the passage. Then, in your Bible reading, a single verse will become significant to you. Why not read it in another translation of the Bible? This translation study will give you a fresh new insight about what God is saying to you.

OBSERVATION STUDY

In observation study, you simply write down what you see. However, you are going to learn to look for certain things as you read through your selected passage of Scripture. I remember when I first got the idea for an observation study. I was reading Hebrews 11 and noticed the word *faith* was repeated many times throughout that chapter. I thought, *Hmmm, I wonder what would happen if I underlined every occurrence and then wrote what I learned about faith from each one.* This was a momentous occasion because I was absolutely astounded at everything I learned. Learning so much from one chapter of the Bible is very rewarding. So where do you begin with observation study? With a word, topic, event, or a character that you notice in your Bible reading during your quiet time.

You may be wondering, *How am I going to know what word, topic, event, or character to study?* In most cases, the answer will be obvious because of what you see in a particular passage of Scripture. In every chapter of the Bible you will notice an emphasis on a topic, a word, a character, or an event. For example, in the first chapters of Luke, you might decide to write down everything you see about Mary (a character in the Bible). Or you might write down everything you see about the birth of Jesus (an event). Almost every chapter in the entire Bible tells you something about God, Jesus, or the Holy Spirit. And almost every chapter in the entire Bible tells you something about humanity. Most importantly, God has a way of showing you what He wants you to see in Scripture. He will actually make a word, topic, character, or event stand out to you as you are in His Word. You don't have to worry about whether you are going to be able to see anything. The Lord will show you the way. Remember what we learned on day 10 of this journey: The Holy Spirit lives in you, and one of His main goals in your life is to teach you from the Bible. And that is really what makes reading and studying the Bible so exciting.

In observation study, as you are reading in a passage of the Bible, ask the question, what do I see about a repeated word (such as faith), a topic (such as suffering), a character (such as Paul, David, God, Jesus, or the Holy Spirit), or an event (such as the birth of Jesus or the Passover)? You will notice that the Psalms are a great place to do an observation study. Almost every psalm includes numerous truths about God. As you read through any psalm, always ask, what do I learn about God in this passage?

Once you know whether it will be a word, topic, character, or event, write the subject of your study at the top of a page in your journal or notebook. Be sure to record the date so you can keep a chronicle of your journey with the Lord. Then note which passage of Scripture you are reading and studying. As you see each truth about a repeated word, topic, character, or event, write out your observations and insights, one by one. If you have time, record the verses related to each insight. Once you have written out all your insights, summarize what you have learned in two or three sentences. Then look at what you have learned and write in one sentence how to apply what you have learned to your own life.

Here are some examples of observation study. As you look at them, you might want to turn to the passage of Scripture and follow along as you look at my observations. Keep in mind that most of what you observe is obvious. You are simply writing out what God says in the verse. In those cases, you will come very close to exactly what I've observed. Other times, you might see something that I didn't notice. There is no right or wrong as long as you stay with the words in the Bible; what you see will be what God is showing you in the passage. Sometimes I will close the application portion with a written prayer. There are no hard-

and-fast rules in this regard. What I share with you are guidelines that you can use and modify as you desire. These are merely ideas that God has shown me in my own adventure with the Lord. Make these studies your own and write what you see to your heart's content! (Detailed steps for an observation study are included in appendix 3.)

OBSERVATION OF A WORD: *FAITH* IN HEBREWS 11:1-3

See figure 2 on page 143. To observe the word *faith* in Hebrews 11:1-3, I would write the following observations:

- v. 1 Faith is the assurance of things hoped for.

- v. 1 Faith is the conviction of things not seen.

- v. 2 People in the past gained approval because of their faith.

- v. 3 By faith I know the world was created by the Word of God.

- v. 3 I know by faith that the visible world was not made by visible things, but invisible.

Summary and conclusions: Faith believes in truths that are invisible to the naked eye. My faith gains approval from God. Even creation is something I believe by faith.

Application in my life: Faith is an important part of my walk with the Lord. I must exercise faith in everything I do. I won't always see what I believe. It is by faith.

OBSERVATION OF A TOPIC: SUFFERING AND TRIALS IN 1 PETER 1:3-7

To observe the topic of suffering and trials in 1 Peter 1:3-7, I would make the following observations (notice that I personalize my observations):

- v. 3 God has great mercy.

- v. 3 God has given me a living hope.

- v. 4 Part of my hope is that I have an inheritance reserved in heaven for me.

- v. 5 I am protected by the power of God through faith.

- v. 6 I can greatly rejoice because of this living hope.

- v. 6 For a little while, sometimes I will necessarily be distressed by various trials.

- v. 7 These trials prove my faith is genuine.

- v. 7 This proof of my faith is more precious than gold.

- v. 7 The trial that tests my faith may be like fire.

- v. 7 The testing of my faith may be found to result in praise and glory and honor at the revelation of Jesus Christ.

Summary and conclusions: It is no accident that I am going through a difficult trial. Sometimes trials are necessary and prove how genuine my faith is. As I stand strong, the result will be praise and glory and honor when Christ is revealed.

Application in my life: I am encouraged to hang in there in my difficulty. I must stand strong by faith and not give up. My endurance proves that my faith is real.

OBSERVATION OF A CHARACTER IN THE BIBLE: GOD IN PSALM 46

From Psalm 46 I would make the following observations about God:

- v. 1 God is my refuge and strength.

- v. 1 God is a very present help to me when I'm in trouble.

- v. 2 Because of that I do not need to fear.

- v. 2 Even in a time of catastrophic change I do not need to fear.

- v. 4 There is a place, a river where gladness can be found. It is the holy dwelling places of the Most High.

- v. 5 When God is in my midst I will not be moved. God will help me.

- v. 7 God is with me. God is my stronghold.

Summary and conclusions: What a comfort this is to me today. Regardless of the trouble I experience or the change I am faced with, I do not need to be afraid because God is my refuge and strength.

Application in my life: What troubles and changes are facing me today! I will remember that God is in my midst, and I need not be afraid or be moved. I will find my shelter and refuge in Him today. Thank You, Lord.

OBSERVATION OF AN EVENT: THE CONVERSION OF PAUL IN ACTS 9

A good example of an event to observe is the conversion of Paul. I would make the following observation in Acts 9:

- v. 1 Paul's name prior to conversion was Saul.

- v. 1 Saul was an enemy of Christians and wanted to have them murdered.

- v. 1 He was such an enemy that he went to the high priest.

- v. 2 He asked for letters that would give him permission to arrest Christians.

- v. 3 As he approached Damascus, a light from heaven flashed around Saul.

- v. 4 He fell to the ground and heard the voice of the Lord.

- v. 5 He asked who it was, and Jesus revealed Himself to Saul.

- v. 6 Jesus told him to go to Damascus.

- v. 7 Those with Saul heard the voice of Jesus but did not see Him.

- v. 8 Saul was blind and was led into Damascus.

- v. 9 For three days he ate and saw nothing.

- v. 10 The Lord spoke to Ananias and told him to go to Paul.

- v. 13-14 Ananias explains that Saul was a real enemy of Christians, so much so that they were terrified of him.

- v. 15 Jesus revealed that Saul is a chosen instrument of the Lord to carry His message to the Gentiles, to kings, and to the sons of Israel.

- v. 16 Jesus also reveals that Saul will suffer for the sake of Jesus.

- v. 17-19 Ananias laid hands on Saul, and Saul regained his sight.

- v. 20 Saul immediately began to tell others that Jesus is the Son of God.

Summary and conclusions: Jesus literally transformed Saul from an enemy to a preacher of the gospel. It was a dramatic, life-changing event.

Application in my life: If Jesus can do that with Paul, He can do it with those in my life who are not saved.

In the adventure of observation study, the sky is the limit. How do I know when to do this particular study? I rely on the Lord to lead me in His Word. When I read the Bible and notice some great observations to be made, I pull out a piece of paper from my journal and begin writing what I see. Just be ready, and whenever you are in the Bible, ask the question, Would this be a good place to look more closely at biblical truth and do an observation study? And here's a secret: Every passage of Scripture contains observations to be made!

TRANSLATION STUDY

John Bunyan was born in 1628 in the heart of England a few years before the start of the English Civil War. Leaving the Church of England, John Bunyan began a preaching ministry that resulted in 12 years of imprisonment, where he completed many of his 60 books. Although in prison, John Bunyan felt he had true freedom because he was able to read the Bible, preach, and sing hymns with no one to stop him. But it was a Bible translation, the Geneva Bible of 1560, that ultimately led John Bunyan to author *The Pilgrim's Progress,* the most widely distributed book outside of the Bible.

You probably have noticed that numerous translations and paraphrases of the Bible are available to you on the market today.

You can explore the spectrum from a literal translation, such as the New American Standard Bible, to a colloquial paraphrase, such as The Message. When you find a verse in the Bible that seems significant to you, looking at that verse in various translations and paraphrases can be extremely helpful. To see the beauty of the many nuances of the original languages of the Bible, see how translators have chosen different English words to portray the Greek and Hebrew. Comparing translations brings excitement to God's Word, opening your vision to verses in a deeper and more meaningful way, perhaps even inspiring your life's ministry.

I love the translation comparisons of Hebrews 11:1 (see figure 3 on page 144). Note how the different phrases and words help you notice more about what Jesus is saying.

- "Now faith is the assurance of things hoped for, the conviction of things not seen" (NASB).

- "Now faith is being sure of what we hope for and certain of what we do not see" (NIV).

- "Now faith is the assurance [the confirmation, the title-deed] of the things [we] hope for, being the proof of things [we] do not see and the conviction of their reality [faith perceiving as real fact what is not revealed to the senses]" (AMP).

Application in my life: My life can be a demonstration of God's truth when I live by faith.

(Detailed steps for a translation study are included in appendix 3.)

Taking time to look at what God is saying in His Word is the most important part of your quiet time each day. Your observation skills will grow and develop as you slow down and look at words, verses, and chapters in the Bible. The more you see, the more curious you will become. Then you will want to know what it all means. Tomorrow you will learn some exciting studies to help you make these new discoveries.

Observation Study

"Be still and know that I am God" (Psalm 46:10 NIV).

Scripture passage: _Hebrews 11:1-6_

Significant word, topic, or character: _Faith_

Observations about a word, topic, or character

Verse	Observations
1	It is the assurance of things hoped for, the conviction of things not seen.
2	It is how men in the past gained God's approval.
3	It is how we understand the invisible things like the creation of the world.
4	It is why Abel's sacrifice was better and it resulted in righteousness.
5	It is why Enoch was pleasing to God and taken without experiencing death.
6	Must have it to please God, believes God exists, rewards us if we seek Him.

Summary and conclusions:

Faith is concerned with the invisible. It is how we understand the invisible, spiritual world. It is how we gain God's approval. Faith results in righteousness. Faith pleases God.

Application in my life:

I must learn to walk by faith because that is what pleases God. Walking by faith today means that I am going to hope in God.

FIGURE 2: OBSERVATION STUDY EXAMPLE

Translation Study

"Study and be eager and do your utmost" (2 Timothy 2:15 AMP).

Selected Verse(s): _Hebrews 11:1_

Write out, word for word, the selected verse(s) for each translation

Translation	Verse(s)
NASB	Now faith is the assurance of things hoped for, the conviction of things not seen.
NIV	Now faith is being sure of what we hope for, and certain of what we do not see.
AMP	Now faith is the assurance (the confirmation, the title-deed) of the things [we] hope for, being the proof of things [we] do not see and the conviction of their reality [faith perceiving as real fact what is not revealed to the senses].

Observations:

Faith is a response to things we hope for and things unseen. It is an assurance, certainty, perceiving as real fact what we cannot see or hear.

Conclusions:

Faith perceives the fact of God's Word, even though my feelings do not always perceive its reality.

Application in my Life:

My life can be a demonstration of God's truth when I live by faith.

FIGURE 3: TRANSLATION STUDY EXAMPLE

DATE:

KEY VERSE: "Angels would have given anything to be in on this!" (1 Peter 1:12 MSG).

FOR FURTHER THOUGHT: Today you had the opportunity to see two ways to dig deeper into the Word of God: observation study and translation study. How do you think these two devotional studies can help you not only study the Word of God but also have the Word of God make its way into your heart and change your life?

MY RESPONSE:

Day Seventeen

ENCOURAGED BY
THE BIBLE

The words of the LORD are pure words,
like silver refined in a furnace on
the ground, purified seven times.

PSALM 12:6 ESV

A world of truth is stored in a word. Looking at a single detail can be the key that unlocks the door to renewal and transformation. Take time to look closely at the words in God's Word. The psalmist has said, "The words of the LORD are pure words, like silver refined in a furnace on the ground, purified seven times" (Psalm 12:6 ESV). Charles Wesley loaned 21-one-year-old George Whitefield *The Life of God in the Soul of Man* by Henry Scougal. In that book Whitefield discovered John 3:3: "Except a man be born again, he cannot see the kingdom of God" (KJV). "When I read this," Whitefield says, "a ray of divine light instantaneously darted in upon my soul; and, from that moment, but not till then, did I know that I must become a new creature." Wesley introduced the book, the book introduced the text, and the words "born again" led George Whitefield to eternal salvation and the kingdom of God. George Whitefield went on to become one of the greatest evangelists of all time and the foremost figure of the powerful revival of the 1700s known as the Great Awakening.

VERSE AND WORD STUDIES

I have always been interested in words. When I first began reading the Bible, I was amazed to discover special dictionaries and word study tools that helped me understand the meaning of the words in the Bible. These tools, such as *Strong's Exhaustive Concordance,* help unlock the meanings because they examine the original languages of the Bible—Hebrew for the Old Testament and Greek for the New Testament. *Strong's* has Hebrew and Greek dictionaries in the back that assign numbers to each English word in the Bible. For more detailed information on how to use an exhaustive concordance, see day 15 in *Six Secrets to a Powerful Quiet Time. Strong's* was the first word study tool I ever used, but I soon found others that unlocked the words of the Bible in even more exciting ways.

My favorite word study tool is the *Key Word Study Bible* by Spiros Zodhiates because it's quick and easy to use and gives many meaningful word definitions. This *Key Word Study Bible* uses the *Strong's* numbering system and assigns *Strong's* numbers to all the key words of the Bible. When you find a verse that is significant to you, choose a word and look for the number next to it. Then, look in the back of the Bible for two dictionaries: a *Strong's* dictionary and "Lexical Aids to the Old and New Testament." Simply find the number and read about your word. The Lexical Aids include many great definitions. For example, Zodhiates defines the Greek word for *blessed (makarios),* used in the beatitudes of Matthew 5:3-11, as possessing the favor of God. He says that the blessed one is "in the world, yet independent of the world. His satisfaction comes from God and not from favorable circumstances."

To use this tool, simply look for the word that interests you in the passage of Scripture you are studying. If it is underlined with a bold underline, it is defined in both dictionaries in the back of the Bible. You will notice to the right of the word is a number—that's the *Strong's* number (see figure 4).

Notice the word *endurance* in verse 3. It is underlined and has the number 5281 to the upper right of the word. That is the *Strong's* number.

Simply look in the back in both dictionaries using the *Strong's* number for your selected word, and you will find your definition (see

> 1 [ᵃJames, a ᵇbond-servant¹⁴⁰¹ of God²³¹⁶ and ᶜof the Lord²⁹⁶² Jesus Christ,⁵⁵⁴⁷ to ᵈthe twelve tribes who are ᴵᴵᵉdispersed abroad, ᶠgreetings.⁵⁴⁶³
>
> 2 ᵃⁱᵐ ᵃConsider it all joy,⁵⁴⁷⁹ my brethren,⁸⁰ when you ᵃᵒˢᵇencounter ᵇvarious₄₁₆₄ ᴵtrials,³⁹⁸⁶
>
> 3 knowing that ᵃthe testing¹³⁸³ of your ᵇfaith⁴¹⁰² produces ᴵᶜendurance.⁵²⁸¹

FIGURE 4: *KEY WORD STUDY BIBLE.*

figure 5). If your word is an unbolded underline, it is defined in the *Strong's* dictionary in the back but not the lexical aids. Most of the key words will have a bold underline and will be defined in both dictionaries. I will often take an extra minute to look up the meaning of a word in my *Key Word Study Bible* and write out what I learn in my journal. In fact, with only an extra five minutes, you can learn the definitions of all the key words in a verse using this amazing word study tool.

> **5281. Hupomone;** patience, endurance as to things of circumstances as contr. to *makrothumia* (3115), long-suffering endurance toward people. From *hupo* (5259), under, and *menó* (3306), to abide. *Hupomoné* is associated with hope (1 Thess. 1:3) and refers to the quality that does not surrender to circumstances or succumb under trial.

FIGURE 5: NEW TESTAMENT LEXICAL AIDS IN THE *KEY WORD STUDY BIBLE*

I have listed the steps to verse study and word study as well as many word study tools in appendix 3 for your reference. In a verse study you look up the meanings to all the key words in a selected verse and record your discoveries in your journal or on the Verse Study page of the *Quiet Time Notebook* (see figure 9 on page 153). Notice in figure 9 how the key words from Hebrews 11:1, *faith, assurance, hoped for,* and *conviction,* are brought to life through Zodhiates' *Key Word Study Bible.* In a word study you will look up the meaning of one word in several word study tools, such as the *Key Word Study Bible, Vine's Expository Dictionary,* and *Strong's Exhaustive Concordance.* Then you record your discoveries in your journal or on the Word Study page of the *Quiet Time Notebook* (see figure 10 on page 154). Notice how the word *faith* from Hebrews 11:1 is amplified by *Strong's, Vine's,* and the *Key Word Study Bible.* These definitions complement one another and are not mutually exclusive, giving a richer view of the text. These kinds of studies yield broader conclusions and more in-depth application to your life. A world of discovery is awaiting you in verse and word studies. (Detailed steps for verse and word studies are included in appendix 3.)

REFERENCE AND TOPICAL STUDIES

Reference and topical studies help you learn what God has to say about specific subjects, truths, ideas, events, and people. The purpose of looking at related verses through a reference or topical study is to take into account the whole counsel of God's Word, clarifying the meaning of the text. When you cross-reference a verse (reference study), you look for other verses in the Bible that are thematically related to the Scripture you are studying. Choose a word or phrase in your verse and look up the references in the margin. To accomplish this kind of study, you need a Bible with cross-references, that is, verse references printed in the side or center margins. To cross-reference a verse, select a favorite phrase and find the letter at the beginning of the selected phrase. Then find the verse number in the margin and the corresponding letter following that number. Next to the letter will be one or more cross-reference verses. Write down the cross-reference verses in your journal or on the Reference Study page (see figure 11 on page 156 for an example of a Reference Study page). Look up each cross-reference in your Bible and write out your insights next to each verse.

For example, if you were to cross-reference "the testing of your faith produces endurance" in James 1:1-3, you would find that one of the cross-references is 1 Peter 1:7 (see figure 6). This cross-reference amplifies the testing of faith, which it is more valuable than gold and will result in praise, glory, and honor at the revelation of Christ. Step-by-step instructions to do a cross-reference study are found in appendix

Testing Your Faith

1 ¹ᵃJames, a ᵇbond-servant of God and ᶜof the Lord Jesus Christ,

¶ To ᵈthe twelve tribes who are ²ᵉdispersed abroad: ᶠGreetings.

2 ¶ ᵃConsider it all joy, my brethren, when you encounter ᵇvarious ¹trials,

3 knowing that ᵃthe testing of your ᵇfaith produces ¹ᶜendurance.

4 And let ¹ᵃendurance have *its* perfect ²result, so that you may be ³ᵇperfect and complete, lacking in nothing.

1:1 ¹Or *Jacob*
²Lit *in the Dispersion* ᵃActs 12:17
ᵇTitus 1:1 ᶜRom 1:1 ᵈLuke 22:30
ᵉJohn 7:35 ᶠActs 15:23
2 ¹Or *temptations* ᵃMatt 5:12; James 1:12
ᵇ1 Pet 1:6
3 ¹Or *steadfastness* ᵃ1 Pet 1:7◄─
ᵇHeb 6:12 ᶜLuke 21:19
4 ¹V 3, note 1
²Lit *work* ³Or *mature* ᵃLuke 21:19 ᵇMatt 5:48; Col 4:12

FIGURE 6: EXCERPT FROM A CROSS-REFERENCE BIBLE

3. A great cross-reference tool is *The Treasury of Scripture Knowledge,* which contains numerous cross-references for verses in the Bible (see figure 7).

A topical study is simply a special version of a reference study, launching out from topics rather than from a particular verse. The topical study helps you learn what the Bible has to say on any topic such as faith, hope, grace, salvation, marriage, children, or love. The best tool for a topical study is *Nave's Topical Bible,* which arranges topics

①️ **James.** Mt 10:3. +*13:55. Mk 3:18. Lk 6:15. Ac 1:13. +12:17. 15:13. 21:18. Ga 1:19. 2:9, 12. Ju *1. **a servant.** Gr. bondservant. Lk 2:29. 16:13. Ac 2:18. 4:29. 16:17. Jn 12:26. Ro 1:1. Ph 1:1. 1 Th 1:9. 2 T 2:24. T 1:1. 1 P 2:16. 2 P 1:1. Re +7:3. **and of.** Jn 15:15. Ro 1:1. 1 C 7:22. Ga 1:10. Ep 6:6. Ph 1:1. Col +3:24. 4:12. 2 T 2:24. 2 P 1:1. Ju 1. Re 1:1. 2:20. **to.** Ex 24:4. 28:21. 39:14. 1 K 18:31. Ezr 6:17. Mt 19:28. 22:30. Ac 26:7. Re 7:4. 21:12. **scattered.** Le 26:33. Dt 4:27. 28:25, 64. 30:3. 32:26. Est 3:8. Ezk 12:15. Am 9:8, 9. Jn +7:35. Ac *2:5, 9-11. *8:1, 4. 15:21. Ga 3:26-29. 1 P *1:1. **greeting.** Ezr 5:7. Ac +15:23. 23:26. 2 T 4:21.

②️ **count.** ver. 12. Mt +*5:10-12. *6:13. Lk 6:22, 23. Ac *5:41. Ro *8:17, 18, 35-37. 2 C √12:9, 10. Ph 1:29. 2:17. Col 1:24. He 10:34. 12:11. 1 P *4:13-16. **all.** √108B, 1 C +13:2. **divers.** Mt 26:41. 1 C +*10:13. He 11:36-38. 1 P 1:6-8. 2 P 2:9. Re 2:10.

③️ **that.** Ro *5:3, 4. +*8:28. 2 C √4:17. 1 P *1:7. **patience.** Ja 5:11. Ro +*2:7. 8:25. +*15:4. Col 1:11. 2 Th 1:4. 3:5. He +*10:36. 12:1. 2 P 1:6.

FIGURE 7: EXCERPT FROM *THE TREASURY OF SCRIPTURE KNOWLEDGE*

in alphabetical order (see figure 8). You can look up any topic and write the verses on your Reference Study page from the *Quiet Time Notebook* or in your journal. Then simply look up every verse and record your insights (see figure 11 on page 156). Notice how the different verses referenced from *Nave's Topical Bible* open up the topic of faith.

Detailed steps for reference and topical studies are included in appendix 3.

> **FAITH.** 2 Sam. 22:31. *As for* God, his way *is* perfect; the way of the LORD *is* tried: he *is* a buckler to all them that trust in him.
> Psa. 5:11. Let all those that put their trust in thee rejoice: let them ever shout for joy, because thou defendest them:
> Psa. 7:1. O LORD my God, in thee do I put my trust: save me from all them that persecute me, and deliver me:
> Psa. 9:9. The LORD also will be a refuge for the oppressed, a refuge in times of trouble. 10. And they that know thy name will put their trust in thee: for thou, LORD, hast not forsaken them that seek thee.
> Psa. 18:30. He *is* a buckler to all those that trust in him.

FIGURE 8: *NAVE'S TOPICAL BIBLE* EXAMPLE

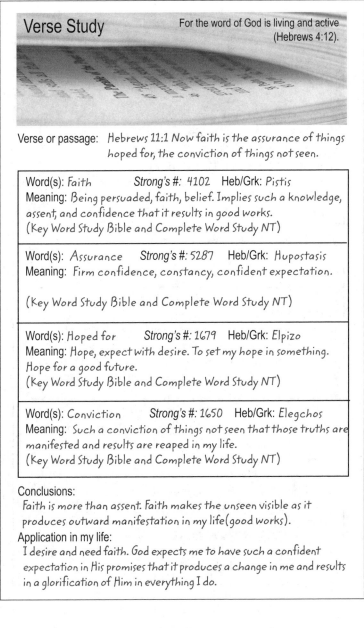

Verse Study

For the word of God is living and active (Hebrews 4:12).

Verse or passage: Hebrews 11:1 Now faith is the assurance of things hoped for, the conviction of things not seen.

Word(s): Faith   Strong's #: 4102   Heb/Grk: Pistis
Meaning: Being persuaded, faith, belief. Implies such a knowledge, assent, and confidence that it results in good works.
(Key Word Study Bible and Complete Word Study NT)

Word(s): Assurance   Strong's #: 5287   Heb/Grk: Hupostasis
Meaning: Firm confidence, constancy, confident expectation.

(Key Word Study Bible and Complete Word Study NT)

Word(s): Hoped for   Strong's #: 1679   Heb/Grk: Elpizo
Meaning: Hope, expect with desire. To set my hope in something. Hope for a good future.
(Key Word Study Bible and Complete Word Study NT)

Word(s): Conviction   Strong's #: 1650   Heb/Grk: Elegchos
Meaning: Such a conviction of things not seen that those truths are manifested and results are reaped in my life.
(Key Word Study Bible and Complete Word Study NT)

Conclusions:
Faith is more than assent. Faith makes the unseen visible as it produces outward manifestation in my life (good works).
Application in my life:
I desire and need faith. God expects me to have such a confident expectation in His promises that it produces a change in me and results in a glorification of Him in everything I do.

FIGURE 9: VERSE STUDY EXAMPLE

Word Study

The word of our God stands forever
(Isaiah 40:8).

Word(s): Faith   Strong's #: 4102   Heb/Grk: Pistis
Other translations: Believe, Trust
Scripture passage for word(s): Hebrews 11

Strong's concordance:

Faith, faithfulness, pledge, proof

Vine's Expository Dictionary:

Believing, trusting, relying

Key Word Study Bible, Complete Word Study NT & OT Dictionary;
Theological Wordbook OT:
Used 6 ways 1. being persuaded, knowledge of, assent to, confidence in God's truth resulting in good works. 2. resulting in
miracles during Christ's time on earth. 3. promising justification
and salvation. 4. Christian religion. 5. Fidelity. 6. Assurance,
proof.

Other Sources: *Linguistic Key to the Greek NT, Wuest's Word Studies,*
Brown's Dictionary of NT Theology, Robertson's Word Pictures,
commentaries, other:
Linguistic Key p. 706: to understand. A mental perception.
Wuest, vol. 2, p. 193: Faith apprehends as real fact what is not
revealed to the senses. It rests on that fact, acts upon it, and is
upheld by it in the face of all that seems to contradict it. Faith
is real sight.
Brown, vol. 1, pp. 593-605: Man's trust presents the possibility
for God to do His work. Not wild enthusiasm. Wrestle with God.
Directed toward reality, deeply involved in the act of living.

FIGURE 10: WORD STUDY EXAMPLE

Word Study Cont'd

Word(s): _Faith_

Other uses in immediate area of study: Used 32 times in Hebrews. 4:2 Word (logos) doesn't profit if not united with faith. 6:11 a believer's foundation. 6:12 necessary to inherit promises— results in patience. 10:22 how we are to draw near. 10:38 how we are to live. 10:39 preserves the soul. 12:2 Jesus is the author and finisher of our faith. 13:7 we are to imitate the faith of our leaders.

Other uses in Old/New Testament: Matt 8:10 centurion is example of great faith. Acts 3:16 our faith is from Jesus and is to be in His name. Rom 1:5 involves obedience 1:12 our faith can encourage others. 1:17 how the righteous are to live 4:9 Abraham an example of faith. 5:1-2 how we are introduced into the grace of God. 12:3 each is allotted a measure of faith. 12:6 we are to exercise our gifts according to our proportion of faith. 14:23 if not from faith then is sin. James 1:3 testing of faith produces endurance. 2:17 true faith accompanied by works. 1 Pet 1:7 Genuine faith more precious than gold.

Conclusions: 1. Faith is how we live and is essential to experiencing all that God promises. 2. Our faith is in God's Word. 3. Faith results in patience, righteousness, justification, salvation, endurance, and the experience of God's grace. 4. I am given a measure of faith and am to exercise gifts accordingly. 5. As a leader, I must demonstrate faith.

Meaning in present study: Hebrews 11 is the hall of fame of faith. Contains numerous examples of those who held strong to promises of God with good works and glorified God.

Application in my life: I am challenged to have a life characterized by biblical faith. This means I am to be obedient to God, patient, and endure all trials and temptations. I can never give up. I must believe God for all things I believe He has called me to do.

Reference Study

"...the grass withers and the flowers fall but the word of the Lord stands forever" (1 Peter 1:24-25 NIV).

Verse/Topic: _Faith_   Scripture: _Hebrews 11:1_

Record observations and insights from the following references related to the selected verse or topic. Define any key words.

Key Word Definitions:
Faith—confidence in divine truth (Taken from Key Word Study Bible.)

_____2 Samuel 22:31_____
Reference
God's way is perfect—He is a refuge (buckler KJV) for those who trust Him.

_____Psalm 51:1_____
Reference
When I trust (put my faith in) God, I can rejoice—He will defend me.

_____Psalm 9:10_____
Reference
Knowing God's name (His ways and character) will help me trust.

_____Romans 1:17_____
Reference
I am to live by faith.

FIGURE 11: REFERENCE OR TOPICAL STUDY EXAMPLE

Reference Study Cont'd

Romans 5:1
Reference

I am justified by faith and, as a result, I am given peace through Christ.

Romans 10:17
Reference

Faith comes from hearing, and hearing from the Word of Christ.

1 Corinthians 2:5
Reference

My faith does not rest in the wisdom of men, but the power of God.

Ephesians 6:16
Reference

Faith is my shield in spiritual warfare.

Summary and conclusions:
1. Trust in God demonstrates my faith.
2. I am to live by faith.
3. Faith comes from hearing the word of Christ.
4. If I want to have faith, I must be in the Word, and come to know God and His ways.
5. Faith is a powerful weapon in spiritual warfare.

Application in my Life:
Lord, today I see how important my demonstration of faith and trust in You is. I see the importance of knowing You in Your Word. Help me to make Your Word a priority.

My Response

DATE:

KEY VERSE: "The words of the LORD are pure words, like silver refined in a furnace on the ground, purified seven times" (Psalm 12:6 ESV).

FOR FURTHER THOUGHT: Today you discovered three new ways to devotionally study the Bible: verse study, word study, and reference or topical study. What was most significant to you as you thought about these different ways to know and love the Bible? What did you learn that you would like to try in your own quiet time?

MY RESPONSE:

Day Eighteen

QUIET TIME—
WEEK THREE:
EXPLORING THE
ROMANCE

This book of the law shall not depart
from your mouth, but you shall
meditate on it day and night.

JOSHUA 1:8

PREPARE YOUR HEART

G. Campbell Morgan, one of the greatest preachers of the nineteenth century, experienced a crisis of faith when he was a young man. He was so desperate that he locked every book he owned in a cupboard, bought a new Bible, and began to read it. He said, "If it be the Word of God, and if I come to it with an unprejudiced and open mind, it will bring assurance to my soul of itself." He canceled every speaking engagement and devoted all his time to studying the Bible. What was the result? He exclaimed, "The Bible found me!" G. Campbell Morgan went on to become one of the great students of the Word of God. He said, "Of all literature none demands more diligent application than that of the Divine Library." His study began at 6:00 AM and lasted without interruption until noon. He read a book of the Bible 40 or 50 times before writing or preaching on it.

G. Campbell Morgan truly discovered the great romance of God and His Word. Everything else paled in comparison to the magnificence of the Bible. Have you made that discovery? As you begin your quiet time, meditate on Psalm 19. Record your most significant insights about the Word of God. Then ask God to speak to your heart today.

READ AND STUDY GOD'S WORD

Throughout the Bible, God encourages His people to give time and effort to be in His Word. Joshua faced a daunting task—he was Moses' successor to lead the people of Israel into the promised land. Read Joshua 1:1-9 and write all that you learn about the Law (God's Word) and what God wanted Joshua to do with the Law.

Look at the following verses and record what you learn about what to do with God's Word:

Colossians 3:16

2 Timothy 2:15

2 Timothy 3:16-17

Summarize in two or three sentences what you have learned about the Word of God today.

Adore God in Prayer

Pray the words of this prayer by Amy Carmichael:

> Let me see Thy face, Lord Jesus,
> Caring not for aught beside;
> Let me hear Thy voice, Lord Jesus,
> Till my soul is satisfied.
>
> Let me walk with Thee, Lord Jesus;
> Let me walk in step with Thee.
> Let me talk with Thee, Lord Jesus;
> Let Thy words be clear to me.
>
> Heavenly music, strength and sweetness,
> Joy of joys art Thou to me;
> O Beloved, my Lord Jesus,
> Let me be a joy to Thee.[1]

Yield Yourself to God

Whenever a new vision is presented to the trusting soul a new crisis is created for that soul, and the soul will either obey and march into larger life, or disobey and turn backward. The man or woman who has the largest, fullest knowledge of Christ is the man or woman who is most conscious that he or she has hardly yet begun to see His glory. The Spirit of God, line upon line, precept upon precept, here a little and there a little, with infinite patience, is forevermore unveiling to the eyes of faithful, watching souls the glory of Christ; and as each new glory is revealed it calls the soul to some new adventure, to some new sacrifice; and wherever there is response to the revelation, realization follows. So by this process of illumination and instruction, we grow up in all things into Him Who is the Head, even Christ Jesus. Every response to light means fuller understanding and enlarged capacity for further revelation. The true Christian life is a growth...There is no exhausting of the light and glory and beauty of Christ...Sanctification is progressive, the Spirit of God patiently leading us from point to point in the life of faith and light and love, and forevermore astonishing us with new unveilings of the glory of our Master. For God, who said, "Light shall shine out of darkness," is the One who has shone in our hearts to give the light of the knowledge of the glory of God in the face of Christ (2 Corinthians 4:6).

G. CAMPBELL MORGAN[2]

When once the Lord has been seen and crowned there is a progressive operation of the Spirit in the life of the believer. The Spirit reveals the Christ to you in some new aspect as you read His Word, as you meditate upon Him, and the moment you see Christ in some new glory, that vision makes a demand upon you. What are you going to do with it? Answer it, obey it, and the Spirit realizes in you the thing you have seen in Christ…The Spirit is always unveiling Christ. Your responsibility and mine if we would cooperate with Him in witness is that we obey when He speaks. When Christ is seen in a new light, the light is calling you to obey its claim. Answer it and you will become the thing you have seen. Deny it and you will sink to lower levels. This is His method, line upon line, here a little and there a little, grace for grace, beauty for beauty.

G. CAMPBELL MORGAN[3]

Fellowship with God, then, as to privilege, is communion with Him; the actuality of friendship and fellowship with God, as to responsibility, is partnership with Him… Fellowship with God means we have gone into business with God, that His enterprises are to be our enterprises …How many people are there in company with whom you can pour out everything in your heart, say everything, say anything? Very, very few…But there is a perfect description of friendship. With your friend you think aloud, there is no restraint; there is no need to keep up an appearance…With God it is my privilege to pour out everything that is in my heart, chaff and grain together, saying anything, saying everything I am thinking. But have we learned that lesson?

Do not we think altogether too often our conversation with God must be that of carefully prepared and often stilted phrasing? I think we never so grieve His heart as when we attempt to speak thus with Him. Conversing with God reaches its highest level when, alone with Him, I pour in His listening ear everything in my heart; and the manner in which I have learned that secret, and live in the power of it, is the measure of the joy and strength of my friendship with God...I can say, and I do say, when alone with God things I dare not say in the hearing of other men. I tell Him all my griefs, and doubts, and fears; and if we have not learned to do so, we have never entered into the meaning of this great truth concerning fellowship. He will take out the grain, and with the breath of friendship blow the chaff away, only we must be honest when we are dealing with Him...Then He will be patient, and loving, and gentle; and out of the infinite love and gentleness of His heart He will speak some quiet word of comfort. How much do we know of this fellowship? How much have we practiced talking to God of everything in our souls?

G. CAMPBELL MORGAN[4]

ENJOY HIS PRESENCE

Do you have a passion to engage and explore this great romance of God and His Word? Will you be a G. Campbell Morgan who spends much time with God in His Word and who enjoys intimate, sweet fellowship with Him? Close your time with the Lord today by writing a prayer expressing all that is on your heart.

REST IN HIS LOVE

"Let the word of Christ richly dwell within you, with all wisdom teaching and admonishing one another with psalms and hymns and spiritual songs, singing with thankfulness in your hearts to God" (Colossians 3:16).

Notes — Week Three

Week Four

EXPERIENCE
THE ROMANCE

༄

Days 19-24

TRANSFORMED BY THE BIBLE

*But prove yourselves doers of the word, and
not merely hearers who delude themselves.*

JAMES 1:22

What you learn from God in His Word will change your life. Isaiah says, "But those who wait for the Lord [who expect, look for, and hope in him] shall change and renew their strength and power" (Isaiah 40:31 AMP). The Lord has a design for your life in mind and intends to transform you from within, making you more like Christ. "For God knew his people in advance, and he chose them to become like his Son" (Romans 8:29 NLT). Paul said, "Don't copy the behavior and customs of this world, but let God transform you into a new person by changing the way you think" (Romans 12:2 NLT). In applying God's Word, you will do it rather than just hear it. James says, "But prove yourselves doers of the word, and not merely hearers who delude themselves" (James 1:22). In the 1600s and 1700s the Puritans were committed followers of Jesus Christ. Their hearts were passionate for Jesus Christ, they were dedicated to the Word of God as the authority for their belief, and they were marked by godliness and purity in their actions and charity. Charles Haddon Spurgeon has been called the heir of the Puritans because of his practice of communing with God using the Bible and countless books written by the Puritans. By the time of his death in 1892, he had almost 7000 Puritan volumes in his library. In essence, Spurgeon spent a lifetime in both character and doctrinal study of the Puritans and the transformation they experienced through the Bible. Their example gave him a great love for the Word of God—so much so that he said, "It is still an El Dorado unexplored, a land whose dust is gold. After thirty-five years I find that the quarry of Holy Scripture is inexhaustible, I seem hardly to have begun to labor in it."[1]

Two devotional studies are especially conducive to helping you get the Word's transforming power into your life: character study and doctrine or ethics study.

CHARACTER STUDY

The Bible is filled with people who met with God, and many of them became heroes of the Christian faith. Alan Redpath points out that "God never flatters His heroes." They had feet of clay and struggled just like you and me. We can learn much from their lives. You will discover that biblical characters are ordinary people who have come into contact with an extraordinary God. If you desire to learn from their lives, you may choose to do a character study. A character study involves using a concordance to find all the passages of Scripture relating to that Bible character, reading them, recording your observations about the person, reading more information about the character in a Bible dictionary or a Bible encyclopedia, summarizing your most important insights, and applying what you have learned to your own life.

DAVID		
father of Jesse, the father of *D*.	Ru 4:17	1732
was born Jesse, and to Jesse, *D*.	Ru 4:22	1732
upon *D* from that day forward.	1Sa 16:13	1732
son *D* who is with the flock."	1Sa 16:19	1732
sent *them* to Saul by *D* his son.	1Sa 16:20	1732
D came to Saul and attended him,	1Sa 16:21	1732
"Let *D* now stand before me;	1Sa 16:22	1732
D would take the harp and play *it*	1Sa 16:23	1732
Now *D* was the son of the	1Sa 17:12	1732
And *D* was the youngest.	1Sa 17:14	1732
but *D* went back and forth from	1Sa 17:15	1732
Then Jesse said to *D* his son,	1Sa 17:17	1732
So *D* arose early in the morning	1Sa 17:20	1732

FIGURE 12: CONCORDANCE EXAMPLE OF DAVID

For example, if you were to do a character study of David, you would discover why God called him "a man after My heart" (Acts 13:22). As you look at the passages listed in your concordance (see figure 12), you learn that David was the son of Jesse (Ruth 4:22), was a shepherd (1 Samuel 16:19), played the harp (1 Samuel 16:23), and was the youngest in his family (1 Samuel 17:14). If you continue on in your concordance, you discover that David defended the Lord's honor (1 Samuel 17:26) and was not afraid to fight Goliath (1 Samuel 17:48). He saw God as the living God (1 Samuel 17:26). He almost always asked God before making a decision (1 Samuel 23:2-4). He did not defend himself when confronted with his own sin, but instead humbled himself before the Lord (1 Samuel 12:13). He loved to sing and praise His Lord and established worship as the priority among the people of Israel (2 Samuel 6:14-18). When you see these character qualities in the life of David, you realize they are desirable goals for your own life. However, there are changes that may be necessary for you to become a man or woman after God's own heart.

Always remember that when you look in the mirror of God's Word at a character in the Bible, the Lord has something in that person's life that He wants you to see. Paul, in speaking about the people of Israel, said, "These things happened to them as an example, and they were written for our instruction, upon whom the end of the ages have come" (1 Corinthians 10:11). What he said about the people of Israel is obviously true of any character in the Bible—they are examples for us to learn from (positively or negatively) and grow. Ask the Lord what He wants you to know and He will show you. Notice that the character study of Noah in figure 13 (page 171) leads to significant principles for your own life. (Detailed steps for a character study are included in appendix 3).

DOCTRINE OR ETHICS STUDY

This study is unique in that you may accomplish it over a period of many years, adding to it with each revisited study. Although this is a more advanced theological study, I've included it here because I want you to know how to do it both now and in the future. As you read and study God's Word, you will notice that the Bible teaches truths about what you believe and how you live your life. These truths relate to both doctrine and ethics. A doctrine is a major teaching of the Bible that forms a Christian's belief system, convictions, character, and manner of life. An ethic is a moral principle or value. The doctrine or ethics study helps you keep track of the truths you discover related to a doctrine or ethic from God's Word.

You may choose to study a doctrine of the Bible such as salvation or the return of Jesus Christ or an important ethical principle related to such things as lying or abortion. You will gradually compile verses on your chosen subject over a period of time as you are in God's Word. Then, when you want to investigate further, you can read about your topic in such tools as a Bible dictionary or encyclopedia, *The Moody Handbook of Theology,* or the *Encyclopedia of Biblical and Christian Ethics.* Record everything you have learned in your journal or on the Doctrine-Ethics Study page for the *Quiet Time Notebook.* Summarize what you have learned. Then write out how you will apply this to your life. Notice how your doctrine or ethics study of the Holy Spirit in figure 14 (page 173) can become your own personal research project that you keep coming back to throughout your lifetime. (Detailed steps for a doctrine or ethics study are included in appendix 3.)

When you apply what you learn in the Bible to your life, resolve to allow the truth of God's Word to make a difference in the kind of life you live. Ask God to make His Word live in you, transform you, and make you more like Jesus.

Character Study

Considering the result
of their conduct, imitate
their faith
(Hebrews 13:7).

Character: *Noah*
Area of study: *Hebrews 11*
Key Scripture Passages: *Genesis 6—9*

Scripture	Observations of life, Insights of character important events, relationship with God
Gen. 6:8	In midst of wickedness on earth, Noah found favor with God.
6:9	Noah a righteous man, blameless in his time Noah walked with God.
6:10	A father of three sons
6:14	Commanded to build an ark
6:22	Noah did everything the Lord commanded him to do.
7:1	Noah was the only one God considered righteous in his time.
7:1-24	Major Event: Noah and his family survived the flood, protected in ark, lone survivors.
8:1	God remembered Noah.
8:10,12	Possessed the ability to wait
8:20	First thing he did after leaving ark: built an altar to the Lord, an aroma soothing to the Lord
9:1	God blessed Noah and his sons, and made them fruitful.
9:11	God established a covenant with Noah.
9:20-24	Noah became drunk with wine—devastating results.
9:29	Noah lived 950 years.

FIGURE 13: CHARACTER STUDY EXAMPLE

Character Study Cont'd   Character: _Noah_

Significant observations of life: _Noah was a father. Had three sons. Was able to build an ark. Lived 950 years._

Major character qualities: _A righteous man. Blameless in his time. Walked with God. Did all God commanded him to do. He was obedient._

Important life events: _Lived in a corrupt world. Experience the flood._

Relationship with God: _Had an intimate relationship with God. He walked with God. Was not afraid to stand blameless, alone in the midst of a corrupt world._

Information from other sources: _New Bible Dictionary, pp. 837-838: He was the last of ten patriarchs. Son of Lamech. Name associated with verb meaning comfort and relief. His life: possessed righteousness that comes from faith. Close communion with God. Covenant with Noah—God promised to never again destroy mankind with a flood._

Most significant principles learned from ___Noah___:
1. _It is possible to walk with God in the midst of a corrupt and evil world even if I am the only one._
2. _It pays to have a life of obedience to God's commands, to be righteous, and to walk with God._

Application in my life:
Corruption around me is no excuse for sin. God expects me to live by faith, with His commands as my standard.

Doctrine or Ethics Study

If you are asked about your Christian hope, always be ready to explain it (1 Peter 3:15 TLB).

Doctrine or ethic: _The Holy Spirit_

Record Scripture references related to selected doctrine/ethic and include any insights gained from your study.

Reference	Insight
John 3:5	Must be born of the Spirit to enter the kingdom of God.
John 14–16	The Holy Spirit is a Comforter given to us by the Father. Abides with us forever. Will be in us. Teaches us all things. Brings Jesus' words to our remembrance. Convicts the world.
Acts 1:5-8	We are to be baptized in the Holy Spirit. Gives us the power to be God's witnesses.
Romans 5:5	The Holy Spirit sheds the love of God abroad in our hearts.
Romans 8	Sets me free from the law of sin and death. Dwells in me. Must have to belong to God. Makes intercession for us according to will of God.

FIGURE 14: DOCTRINE OR ETHICS STUDY EXAMPLE

My Response

DATE:

KEY VERSE: "But prove yourselves doers of the word, and not merely hearers who delude themselves" (James 1:22).

FOR FURTHER THOUGHT: What Bible character has helped you the most in your life? What was it about your favorite Bible character that challenged you? Who would you like to study in the future? What did you learn today that you would like to apply in your quiet time? What area of your life is the greatest challenge for you? Can you think of a verse or passage in the Bible that you could apply to your situation today?

MY RESPONSE:

THOSE WHO HAVE GONE BEFORE US

*A wise teacher's words spur students
to action and emphasize important
truths. The collected sayings of the wise
are like guidance from a shepherd.*

ECCLESIASTES 12:11 NLT

lassic Christian literature and reference works can unleash the treasure of the Word like the counsel of a wise friend. "A wise teacher's words spur students to action and emphasize important truths. The collected sayings of the wise are like guidance from a shepherd" (Ecclesiastes 12:11 NLT). William E. Channing said that "in the best books, great men talk to us, give us their most precious thoughts, and pour their souls into ours." The writer of Hebrews encourages us to "remember those who led you, who spoke the word of God to you; and considering the result of their conduct, imitate their faith" (Hebrews 13:7). Those who have gone before us who have known the depth and treasure of God's Word can continue to speak to us today if we will meditate on their words.

Not so long ago boxes surrounded me like so many mountains to climb. The moving company was arriving in two days, and my books were still lining their shelves, yet to be catalogued and certainly not tucked away. I stared down into the box I was working on, and a bright red book with torn edges stared right back at me: *The Silver Lining* by John Henry Jowett. Ignoring my deadline, I reached for the book. Drawing it toward me, it fell open to a page with an underlined quote, "If He purposes my perfection, then all my circumstances will be made to conspire to the accomplishment of His will." One page led to another until I had consumed 45 minutes in a spontaneous quiet time with one of the great writers of the nineteenth century.

The next morning, in my quiet time, I discovered that John Henry Jowett was a pastor in England in the late 1800s and a contemporary of G. Campbell Morgan, one of the great expository preachers of the era. In subsequent weeks, this discovery of Jowett led me to explore rare and used bookstores, collecting as many of his works as I could find. I decided to make that year a John Henry Jowett year and meditate on what he had written. Having compiled a small library of John Henry Jowett, I can truly say that he has become a friend, a mentor, and one of my favorite Bible teachers. I love what he says in *The Best of John Henry Jowett:*

> The God of peace shall be with you. And that is everything. If the King is present at the table, a crust is a feast. If the Lord is on the battlefield, then amid all the surrounding turbulence there is a centre of peace. When the God of peace is in the life there is a chamber of which the sound of warfare never comes.

John Henry Jowett shows me how to think more deeply about what God says in the Bible. And that is the power of a good book. It can lead you deeper into your relationship with God Himself.

And now, what about you? Who is your John Henry Jowett? What authors remain hidden to your soul, waiting to be discovered in your quiet time? What Bible study tools gather dust, hoping to enhance your relationship with the Lord? A person's library speaks volumes about the person. S. Weir Mitchell says, "Show me the books he loves, and

I shall know the man far better than through mortal friends." Charles Haddon Spurgeon, the prince of preachers, was known for his collection of Puritan books. He began his library at the age of six years old and "ransacked bookstalls and kept an eagle eye on booksellers' catalogs for any he did not possess. His discernment in these books became as delicate as a china-collector's."[1] Spurgeon's library, containing 12,000 volumes (including 7000 Puritan books), many marked with his own hand, is housed in Liberty, Missouri, at William Jewell College.[2]

Another great collector of books was Wilbur M. Smith, born in 1894, and one of the founding professors of Fuller Theological Seminary. He was considered one of the preeminent experts in Christian books in the twentieth century and wrote *A Treasury of Books for Bible Study.* Many scholars feel that perhaps his most valuable contributions were the extensive bibliographies included in his books. He was especially passionate that pastors and leaders choose their books well. He recommended that every pastor take *A Man of the Word,* the biography of G. Campbell Morgan written by Jill Morgan, and read it behind a locked door alone with God. Wilbur Smith's library grew to a vast 25,000 volumes, and some of it is housed as a special collection at Fuller Seminary in Pasadena, California.

WHERE TO BEGIN

I have always loved books and have been reading since I was four years old. In fact, I used to read books under the covers late at night with a flashlight until my mother would poke her head in the door and say, "Lights out." While in college, after surrendering my life to Christ, I began collecting books in earnest. My favorite authors include A.W. Tozer, G. Campbell Morgan, Andrew Murray, Amy Carmichael, Hannah Whitall Smith, John Henry Jowett, and Oswald Chambers. For book recommendations, see my list in the appendix in *Six Secrets to a Powerful Quiet Time.* My guideline in choosing books and Bible study tools is directed by Hebrews 13:7 as I look for authors who accurately speak the Word of God, are faithful to Him, and live godly lives.

Your Bible study library is part of your overall quiet time library and includes your Bible, your *Quiet Time Notebook* or journal, and Bible study tools. I would love for you to be outfitted to accomplish any of the devotional studies I have described. To have a well-rounded Bible study library, you will need the following tools:

- cross-reference Bible

- exhaustive Bible concordance corresponding to your Bible translation

- study Bible, such as the NIV Study Bible

- Bible dictionary or encyclopedia, such as the *New Bible Dictionary*

- Bible atlas, such as the Zondervan *NIV Atlas of the Bible*

- one-volume commentary, such as the *New Bible Commentary*

- word study tool, such as the Hebrew-Greek *Key Word Study Bible*

In appendix 4 I have recommended some Bible study tools. The key is choosing the correct Bible study tool for each devotional study. Keep in mind you do not need to purchase all of the books I describe, and certainly you will not purchase them all at once. I have taken years to develop my Bible study library. I simply gave my family and friends a list of books I would love to have someday, and I received them over the years on birthdays and other holidays.

A good Bible study tool for your devotional Bible study can become a lifetime investment for spiritual growth. One day in my quiet time I was studying Jesus' travels from Jerusalem to Bethany in Matthew 21 ("And He left them and went out of the city to Bethany, and spent the night there" Matthew 21:17). I reached for my *Zondervan NIV Atlas of the Bible* and turned to a map of Palestine, discovering that Bethany is south of Jerusalem, within walking distance. To discover more about Bethany, I opened the *Archaeological Encyclopedia of the Holy Land* edited by Avraham Negev, and I discovered that Bethany was excavated from 1949 to 1953 by S.J. Saller. Unearthed remains include houses, tombs, winepresses, cisterns, silos, and pottery. This brought to my mind that Bethany was a real place that existed during the time that Jesus walked on the earth. A place where Jesus visited His friends Mary, Martha, and Lazarus. And a place where Jesus went often to rest.

I wondered what the area looked like to Jesus as He walked from Jerusalem to Bethany. I pulled out my *New Bible Dictionary* and found that this ground on the far side of the Mount of Olives is covered with fruit trees and waving grain, a wonderful place to fellowship with good friends. Next I explored Frank E. Gaebelein's *Expositor's Bible Commentary*, uncovering the historical background of the passage as well as a bibliography for further study. The entire passage was alive through my Bible study tools.

I encourage you to take great care as you build your Bible study library, endeavoring to add books by those men and women of God who have gone before us and who have loved God and His Word. I'll never forget the day I was investigating the annual book sale at Bethel Theological Seminary in San Diego. My find was an unassuming small book titled *The Story of David Livingstone*. When I opened to the flyleaf, I discovered the former owner of the book, whose signature was written in her own handwriting, was none other than Henrietta C. Mears. Henrietta Mears is one of my heroes of the Christian faith. She wrote her own Sunday school curriculum and was a woman of influence in her day. As a founder of Forest Home Conference Center in California, she fed into the lives of such men as Dr. Richard Halverson, Dr. Bill Bright, and Dr. Billy Graham. Who is your Henrietta Mears? Who is your Charles Spurgeon? Who is your John Henry Jowett? May we live our lives with the same passion and faithfulness as those who have gone before us so that others who follow us will be led to Christ.

My Response

DATE:

KEY VERSE: "A wise teacher's words spur students to action and emphasize important truths. The collected sayings of the wise are like guidance from a shepherd" (Ecclesiastes 12:11 NLT).

FOR FURTHER THOUGHT: Who is your favorite hero of the Christian faith? Who has influenced you in your own life with the Lord? What is your favorite book, and how has it made a difference in your life? What is your favorite Bible study tool, and how has it helped you understand the Bible? What Bible study tool would you like to try using in your quiet time?

MY RESPONSE:

Day Twenty-One

COMMUNION WITH JESUS

I have called you friends, for all things
that I have heard from My Father
I have made known to you.

JOHN 15:15

J esus is the best Friend you will ever have. He is the only One who will never let you down. He will never leave you. He says, "Greater love has no one than this, that one lay down his life for his friends. You are My friends if you do what I command you. No longer do I call you slaves, for the slave does not know what his master is doing; but I have called you friends, for all things that I have heard from My Father I have made known to you" (John 15:13-15). Friendship with Jesus includes entering into the privilege of communion with Him. You have spent the last four days looking at many ways to spend more time with the Bible so that it might make its way into your heart. The result will be face-to-face communion with Jesus. And that is really the purpose of knowing and loving the Bible—that you will come into a deeper relationship with the Lord. As the Word becomes more personal to you, even so will the Lord become more personal to you. The Bible is filled with words of life for you. Your greatest times of communion with Jesus will be when you open the pages of your Bible.

Communion with Jesus includes times of intimate companionship with Him. A servant is only acquainted with his Master, but a friend is intimate with the Master. A servant only serves the Master, but a friend shares in His life. Most people have barely scratched the surface of the intimacy that is possible with Jesus. He says in Revelation 3:20 (ESV), "Behold, I stand at the door and knock. If anyone hears my voice and opens the door, I will come in and eat with him, and he with me." Have you ever shared a meal with a good friend? You enjoy an openness and freedom to share whatever is on your heart and the happiness of being in that friend's presence. That is what the Lord is talking about here. He wants you to share His life and enjoy intimate communion!

Communion with Jesus also includes times of supplication with Jesus—you can ask Him for anything. In fact, He expects you to come to Him and is waiting to hear the requests from the deepest recesses of your heart. He says, "If you abide in Me, and My words abide in you, ask whatever you wish, and it will be done for you" (John 15:7). Jesus commended the centurion's great faith for asking for the healing of his servant (Matthew 8:5-13).

Communion with Jesus also includes times of enjoyment with Him. This may mean moments of laughing together with Him, especially in private moments as you observe those things that bring joy to His heart and your heart. I'll never forget receiving some amazing news about the publication of one of my books by e-mail. I just stopped, smiled, looked up and said, "That was You, Lord, wasn't it! Only You could have accomplished such an incredible work as that! Thank You, Lord!" Jesus said, "These things I have spoken to you so that My joy may be in you, and that your joy may be made full" (John 15:11).

Communion with Jesus includes times of celebration with Him. David said, "Therefore, I will celebrate before the LORD" (2 Samuel 6:21). I especially love celebrating some of the high moments in life with Jesus. Just this past six months, I realized one of the dreams of my life with the publication of *Six Secrets to a Powerful Quiet Time*.

Seeing it in the bookstore for the first time spurred me to make an impromptu date with Jesus for lunch. And as I sat alone with Jesus on a terrace overlooking the desert mountains, I thanked Him for His great provision. When big things happen, I get the most joy out of my celebration time alone with the Lord because I recognize Him at work.

Communion with Jesus includes times of suffering together. It is called "the fellowship of His sufferings" in Philippians 3:10. Years ago, I was in a head-on collision in Dallas, Texas. As I was in the emergency room, lying on the table with a big gash on one side of my head, I thought about the crown of thorns pressed into Jesus' head. I had a tremendous sense that Jesus was right there with me and that He knew my pain. He was a comfort to me in that trauma. We were suffering together. I was not alone.

When you face a trial, you are not alone. The Lord suffers with you, and He will give you strength. You and the Lord will mourn and grieve together. "Weep with those who weep," Paul said in Romans 12:15. We know from John 11:35 that when Lazarus died, "Jesus wept." Tozer says that we must remember the Lord is a Person, and in the depth of His nature, He has feelings. The Lord is sensitive and extremely emotional in the depth of His being. He wears His heart on His sleeve. He is not coy and distant. He is sensitive both to you and to the situation. This is not weakness in God. It is the love, compassion, and kindness of God. I love His mercy and grace that leads Him to weep with me.

Communion with Jesus includes times of ministry with Him. The way I look at it, the Lord and I work hard in ministry together—I very much have the sense of fellowship with Him in ministry. I am available, and He is able. He gives me ideas for ministry that I write in my journal and implement through the ministry of my friends at church and at Quiet Time Ministries. And He will give you strength to minister in the area where He has called you to serve. "Faithful is He Who calls you, and He also will bring it to pass" (1 Thessalonians 5:24). If He calls you to speak, He will give you what you need to present those messages. If He wants you to lead a Bible study, He will show you the way to do it. If He wants you to encourage a friend, He will give you the uplifting words. The Lord Jesus can do anything! Always remember, He is the Lord of the universe. There is nothing that He does not know how to do. I often laugh when I think of the most difficult class for me in seminary—eschatology. I remember asking the Lord for brilliance because I surely needed it. And I often pray for brilliance because we are in union together. He gives me what I need to accomplish what He asks me to do.

Communion with Jesus includes times of renewal and revival with Him. Your heart will burn with a contagious love that will spread everywhere. The two on the road to Emmaus were downcast and despairing because they had witnessed Jesus' crucifixion. Then they met a stranger on the road who opened up the Scriptures to them and, beginning with Moses and all the prophets, explained to them the things concerning Jesus in the Scriptures. When these two men realized that it was Jesus, they said, "Were not our hearts burning within us while He was speaking to us on the road, while He was explaining the Scriptures to us?" (Luke 24:32). Then they returned to Jerusalem and shared what happened to them. Your heart will burn with love for Jesus as you commune with Him, and you will have an impact on your world.

Finally, communion with Jesus includes time of fellowship with Him, just basking in His presence. These are usually times of worship, when you are sensing who He is—His majesty, love, joy, strength, and power. Become a worshipper of Jesus, your Lord and your dearest Friend. I love these times because they often happen in response to times in His Word. They happen in response to times when I listen to inspiring worship music. Sometimes it's in my car. Sometimes in my study. Sometimes as I close my eyes to go to sleep at night. These times of communion with the Lord Jesus, for me, are very private and intimate. For me, this is a communion reserved only for Him. Although at times I am moved to tears in a group, my most outward and unreserved times of worship happen when I am alone with the Lord, and they can be incredibly sweet and beautiful.

I have enjoyed this love relationship with the Lord and feel as though it has only just begun even though I have known Him now for more than 30 years. Every time I open the pages of the Bible, I sense that the Lord is waiting there to meet with me. When I look up a word in my *Key Word Study Bible,* I acknowledge that the Lord wants to teach me something about that word. When I research a topic in my *Nave's*

Topical Bible, I trust that the Lord wants to reveal something important to me about that topic. When I examine a character in the Bible, I know that the Lord wants to show me something from that life. Every time I open the pages of the Bible, I come face-to-face with my Lord. That intimacy grows with each passing day and builds in me a commitment to Him that this world cannot touch. The Lord will do the same for you when you study His Word.

During World War II, Korean imperial oppressors appointed a day for the mass pilgrimage to a pagan shrine, where everyone was commanded to worship or face merciless torture. One young Christian girl, a music teacher at a Christian school, threw herself to the floor and with great sadness poured her heart out to Jesus. This lone Christian girl could hear only Jesus' words: "I am the way, the truth, the life." Later, as Esther Ahn Kim made her way up the mountain with hundreds of others, she looked at the sky and prayed, *I will proclaim that there is no other God besides You. This is what I will do for Your holy name.* She trembled as she began reciting Scripture out loud. "My sheep hear My voice, and I know them, and they follow Me; and I give eternal life to them, and they will never perish; and no one will snatch them out of my hand. My Father, who has given them to Me, is greater than all; and no one is able to snatch them out of the Father's hand." Finally at the shrine, before a great crowd and military police, Esther Ahn Kim began reciting the Lord's Prayer because she was so afraid. And then came the command to bow and worship the pagan gods. The enormous crowd followed the shouted order by bending the upper half of their bodies solemnly and deeply. Only Esther Ahn Kim remained standing, looking straight at the sky. She was a young, frightened girl who could not do anything but stand because she was not alone. There was One who stood with her, the Overcomer in every situation in life and the greatest Friend she would ever have. Esther Ahn Kim's action that day on the mountain was the beginning of a journey that led to years in prison before her eventual release. God used her to bring the light of Jesus Christ to the darkness of hundreds of thousands of prisoners during World War II. She was never alone—Jesus was with her every step of the way through His Word and Spirit.

Oh, what a priceless privilege it is to have communion with Jesus.

The words of the hymn writer ring true: "I'd rather have Jesus than silver or gold. I'd rather be His than have riches untold…I'd rather have Jesus than anything this world affords today." Someone has said, "A friend is the one who comes in when the whole world has gone out." Jesus stood with Esther Ahn Kim on the day she refused to worship the pagan gods. And as Stephen was being stoned to death by the Jews, and the heavens opened, Jesus was not sitting—He was standing at the right hand of God. Paul said to Timothy that at his first defense no one supported him; all deserted him, but the Lord stood with him and strengthened him. Regardless of what happens, the Lord stands with you in His Word!

> I come to the garden alone
> while the dew is still on the roses,
> and the voice I hear falling on my ear,
> the Son of God discloses.
>
> He speaks, and the sound of His voice
> is so sweet the birds hush their singing,
> and the melody that He gave to me
> within my heart is ringing.
>
> And He walks with me, and He talks with me,
> and He tells me I am his own;
> and the joy we share as we tarry there,
> none other has ever known.
>
> *"In the Garden"*
> C. AUSTIN MILES

My Response

DATE:

KEY VERSE: "I have called you friends, for all things that I have heard from My Father I have made known to you" (John 15:15).

FOR FURTHER THOUGHT: What truth about Jesus meant the most to you today? In what way do you need Him in your present circumstance of life? Will you take some time right now, close your eyes, and imagine that He is with you to comfort and encourage you? Write a prayer to Him expressing all that is on your heart.

MY RESPONSE:

Day Twenty-Two

WHEN YOU SEE THE
FACE OF GOD

*And He said, "I Myself will make all My
goodness pass before you, and will proclaim
the name of the LORD before you."*

EXODUS 33:19

The face of God shines from every page of the Bible. As you live in the Bible, you will come to know God's ways and character. You will see His heart. You will see Him the way Paul described in 1 Corinthians 13:12 (CEV): "Now all we can see of God is like a cloudy picture in a mirror." He promises that we will "behold (in the Word of God) as in a mirror the glory of the Lord" (2 Corinthians 3:18 AMP). The mirror shows us the truth about God, His character, and His ways. Moses made some bold requests of God. He said, "Let me know Your ways that I may know You" (Exodus 33:13). Then he cried out to God, "I pray You, show me Your glory" (Exodus 33:18), and God answered by saying, "I Myself will make all My goodness pass before you, and will proclaim the name of the LORD before you" (Exodus 33:19).

What a day it must have been when the Lord passed in front of Moses and proclaimed His name to him (Exodus 34:6-7). We learn from Scripture that "Moses immediately fell to the ground and worshiped" (Exodus 34:8 NLT). Every view God gives you in the Bible calls for a corresponding response in your own life. Moses saw the greatness of God and immediately worshipped. What will be your response?

Take a Spiritual Inventory

From time to time throughout the year I take a quick spiritual inventory to discover how the truths I have learned about God are being applied in my life. A spiritual inventory is something you might think through once a month or four times a year. Asking questions like these helps keep you accountable to what God is teaching you as you walk with Him. Then I like to write my discoveries in my journal. You might ask the following questions in your spiritual inventory:

- Am I walking by faith?
- Do I love others like God loves me?
- Do I live a holy life?
- Am I trusting God?
- Do I hope in the Lord?
- How is my quiet time with the Lord?
- How well do I know God?
- Would God call me a man or woman after His own heart?
- Do I seek the Lord?
- Do I ask God before I make decisions?
- How well do I know God's Word?

Make a Spiritual Response

Once you have taken this spiritual inventory, consider the appropriate response. In some cases, you may need to confess a sin (agree with God that you have missed the mark—1 John 1:9), or you may need to change the direction of your life (repent or reconsider—2 Peter 3:9). If you have really gone your own way and are far from the Lord, sometimes it is helpful to write out every sin in your life that comes to your mind on a piece of paper. I learned this many years ago from a speaker in Campus Crusade for Christ and have applied it more than once in my own life. Once you have made your list, write the words of 1 John 1:9 across the list: "If we confess our sins, He is faithful and righteous to forgive us our sins and to cleanse us from all unrighteousness." Then, know that you are forgiven because of the blood Jesus shed on the cross for your sins. Rip that piece of paper into a thousand pieces and throw it away.

The Lord may show you that He wants you to go in a new direction of life or ministry, such as when He moved my husband and me from San Diego to Palm Desert. This led to a whole new chapter for Quiet Time Ministries. "The mind of man plans his way, but the LORD directs his steps" (Proverbs 16:9). At these times, your response is to surrender and say, Yes, Lord. Then ask Him to show you the way.

You may discover someone in your life who needs encouragement. In fact, the Lord will give you all kinds of ideas to express His love to others (1 John 4:11-12). You may write a note to someone or take a friend to lunch. He may show you a need and ask you to meet it in some way. First John 4:11 says, "Beloved, if God so loved us, we also ought to love one another."

From your time of spiritual inventory, you may see that you need to go deeper in God's Word and spend more quiet time with Him. God told Joshua, "This book of the law shall not depart from your mouth, but you shall meditate on it day and night, so that you may be careful to do according to all that is written in it; for then you will make your way prosperous, and then you will have success" (Joshua 1:8). The very fact that you are on this 30-day journey reveals your own heartfelt response to meet Him in His Word.

Another vital response to God, essential to your spiritual growth, is to form resolves and convictions based on what you see in His Word. Once you have matched your life to what you see in the mirror of God's Word, decide what you're going to do about it. You can choose to ignore it. Some people do exactly that. Remember that God gives you truth from His Word for your good, that you might become a partaker of His divine nature—that is, that you might experience Him for yourself (see 2 Peter 1:4). If you examine the psalms of David closely, you will notice that he often formed resolves and convictions. He spent considerable time restating what he knew to be true about God. Then he made a conviction, such as "I will sing praises to you, for you, O God, are my fortress, the God who shows me steadfast love" (Psalm 59:17 ESV). "My heart will not fear...in spite of this I shall be confident" (Psalm 27:3). Forming a conviction simply means that you look at God and His Word and say, "Because of what I see and know to be true, I will do this...or I won't do that..." Some would say that's legalism, but it's not. It's love—love for God Himself.

Set Spiritual Goals

Paul encourages us to "run in such a way that you may win" (1 Corinthians 9:24). He points out that you never run without aim; you must run in a direction with a goal. Fellowship with the Lord prompts a response from your heart. Summarize your spiritual aspirations into specific goals:

- Write a spiritual goal for the year—the one thing you would like to see happen spiritually in your life.

- Choose a verse for the year that will form the foundation for your goal.

- Choose a word for the year that is descriptive of your goal and verse and that you can meditate on all year long.

This process of spiritual inventory and spiritual response has been invaluable to me as I have come to know God more and more in recent trials. Over the last few years, as I spent much time in the Word and saw so many powerful truths about God, I realized that I needed to trust God more. I realized I worried a great deal, but God certainly was not worried. I thought, *If God is who I know Him to be, and the Word is true, why am I anxious and worried?* Then, during that time, my mother suffered a terrible accident, and I spent many days and nights taking care of her to help her get well. I prayed, *Lord, I want to trust You more.*

And so I chose the word *trust* as my word for the year. Then I chose the verses in Proverbs 3:5-6—"Trust in the LORD with all your heart and do not lean on your own understanding. In all your ways acknowledge Him, and He will make your paths straight." Then I set my spiritual goal for the year—to trust God completely in all circumstances. Every day I thought of the word *trust,* and one day in my quiet time the Lord gave me an acrostic for the word: Total Reliance Under Stress and Trial.

God is everywhere in the Bible, revealing Himself to you. He wants to show you Himself. He wants to speak to you about what He is doing in your life. He wants to let you know how He operates, how He works in circumstances. He wants to reveal to you His desires for you as one of His own—the things that please Him, the kinds of qualities He wants to build in your life. When you see God face-to-face, the vision leads to transformation, causing a response in your own heart. Once you catch a glimpse of His face, you will never be the same. Moses removed his shoes when he saw the burning bush because he was on holy ground. And you too will worship.

My Response

DATE:

KEY VERSE: "And He said, 'I Myself will make all My goodness pass before you, and will proclaim the name of the LORD before you'" (Exodus 33:19).

FOR FURTHER THOUGHT: Describe what it means to see the face of God. How does the Bible help you see His face? In what ways have you seen His face? Will you take some time today for a spiritual inventory and think through the questions in today's reading? Will you ask God to give you a word and a verse for the year?

MY RESPONSE:

Day Twenty-Three

PRAYING THE BIBLE

Don't copy the behavior and customs of this world, but let God transform you into a new person by changing the way you think. Then you will know what God wants you to do.

ROMANS 12:2 NLT

The Bible makes you think in a new way. And that new thinking transforms your life. In Romans 12:1-2 (NLT), Paul says, "And so, dear brothers and sisters, I plead with you to give your bodies to God. Let them be a living and holy sacrifice—the kind he will accept. When you think of what he has done for you, is this too much to ask? Don't copy the behavior and customs of this world, but let God transform you into a new person by changing the way you think. Then you will know what God wants you to do, and you will know how good and pleasing and perfect his will really is."

When you are knowing and loving the Bible, experiencing God in His Word, God Himself changes your pattern of thinking. You become a completely new person—His person in the world. His Word impacts your heart and your life, causing you to discover profound truths that change the way you think and that ultimately transform your life.

You discover God is in control. You will experience within yourself an acceptance, an approval, and a testing of God's will. You discover that God is in charge of the world—not people, not the church, but God alone. You remember that God is who He says He is, and you begin to experience the great adventure of knowing Him. "Yours, O LORD, is the greatness and the power and the glory and the victory and the majesty, indeed everything that is in the heavens and the earth; Yours is the dominion, O LORD, and You exalt Yourself as head over all" (1 Chronicles 29:11).

You discover God is at work in your life. You see how God is working all things together. You realize God is at work in the lives of those around you as you begin to understand God and His ways. Things you thought were coincidences stand out as the work of God. You begin to participate in and experience God's plan for your life. "For I am confident of this very thing, that He who began a good work in you will perfect it until the day of Christ Jesus" (Philippians 1:6).

You discover God has good intentions toward you. As you daily live in God's eternal desires, plans, and purposes, you begin to walk with conviction every step of the way. You discover that the will of God for you is good, acceptable (you will accept it and receive it), and perfect. "And do not be conformed to this world, but be transformed by the renewing of your mind, so that you may prove what the will of God is, that which is good and acceptable and perfect" (Romans 12:2).

You discover God has a purpose for you. As you are transformed by the Word, you begin to experience the supernatural life of the great adventure of knowing God. " 'For I know the plans that I have for you' declares the LORD, 'plans for welfare and not for calamity to give you a future and a hope'" (Jeremiah 29:11). God gives you a supernatural ability to trust and to be encouraged as He carries out His purposes in your life. The change you have experienced from within results in a change in the world around you as God works out His purposes. You may have appeared to be down, but you were never out because of the influence of God's Word in your life. And this is where your transformation teaches the world. As you become more and more like

Christ, you begin to forgive others. You dare to do mighty things in the strength and power of God, things you would never have done before. You love the unlovable, are patient with difficult people and difficult situations, trust that God is at work even when you can't see circumstances changing right away. All these things take shape as you respond in prayer to what you see in the Word.

You discover the beauty of God's design. This is where you delight in God's eternal desires, plans, and purposes. "For we are His workmanship, created in Christ Jesus for good works, which God prepared beforehand so that we would walk in them" (Ephesians 2:10). You see the design and say *yes!* In the midst of what you are going through you can say yes to God even if you don't understand. Your words echo the words of the psalmist: "Wonderful are your works, and my soul knows it very well" (Psalm 139:14). All of this happens as part of your prayer response to God's Word. Ultimately, you agree that God is bringing about His plans and purposes, and you cooperate with Him in them. Yes, you will experience lots of hills and valleys. But the view is breathtaking. It is extraordinary and supernatural.

HOW TO PRAY GOD'S WORD

You may be wondering how this experience of discovery, transformation, and renewal can be yours. How can you, as Wuest says in his translation of Romans 12:1-2, change your outward expression to one that comes from within? How can you actually renew your mind and change the way you think? By praying the Bible. In this way, your prayers are inhabited by the will of God. God's will is found in His Word, the Bible. Only there can you be assured that you are praying in accordance with God's eternal desires, plans, and purposes. When you pray the Word, you will find that sweet place of surrender and reckless abandonment to the will of God.

Paul included numerous prayers in his letters to the churches. You will also discover other prayers throughout the Bible, such as Hannah's prayer in the temple (1 Samuel 1), allowing a glimpse into the prayer lives of some of the great saints of the Old and New Testaments. But the prayerbook of the Bible is Psalms. Try writing your own psalm in your journal as a prayer to the Lord. Always direct the words to God. For example, starting with Psalm 18:30-36, you might pray this way:

> Lord, Your way is blameless, Your Word is tried. You are a shield to me when I take refuge in You. Who is God, but You? Who is a rock, except You? You gird me with strength and make my way blameless. You make my feet like hinds' feet, and set me upon my high places. You train my hands for battle, so that my arms can bend a bow of bronze. You have also given me the shield of Your salvation, and Your right hand upholds me; and Your gentleness makes me great. You enlarge my steps under me, and my feet have not slipped.

As you begin praying the psalms, you will discover how perfectly designed they are for prayer. In the psalms, you will find words to praise and worship God. He loves hearing His Word and watches over it to perform it (Jeremiah 1:12). His stamp of approval is on His Word because it is filled with His ways, His plans, His purposes. You will notice that as I wrote out the psalm as a prayer, I personalized it. Make the Word your own by personalizing it as you pray it to the Lord.

Another place to find wonderful prayers is in Paul's letters. You might pray Colossians 1:9-12 for your friends or family:

> I pray that Elizabeth (or whoever is the object of your prayers that day) may be filled with the knowledge of Your will in all spiritual wisdom and understanding, so that she will walk in a manner worthy of You, to please You in all respects, bearing fruit in every good work and increasing in the knowledge of You, that she would be strengthened with all power, according to Your glorious might, for the attaining of all steadfastness and patience; that she would joyously give thanks to You, for You have qualified her to share in the inheritance of the saints in light.

When you pray a prayer such as this, you know it is according to the will of God because it is the Word of God. Therefore, according to 1 John 5:14-15 you can know that you have what you asked for. Your prayer will be answered.

Do you see how exciting praying the Bible can be in your own life? When you pray God's Word, your prayers become strategic and powerful in the work of God in your life and in the lives of your friends, your church, your community, your nation, and your world. One person who is committed to the Lord in prayer and in His Word has the opportunity to become an officer in the army of the Lord. Regardless of how insignificant and unknown you may think you are, you are on the front lines if you are praying God's Word on behalf of people and nations. I believe that when we get to heaven, we are going to see that the real partners in God's work in this world were those whose names we never knew and whose faces we never saw. Oh, may each of us be one of those people. God says in 2 Chronicles 16:9 that His eyes are searching "to and fro throughout the earth that He may strongly support those whose heart is completely His." What a powerful encouragement to wholeheartedly pray in response to His Word. (See appendix 5 for more prayers in the Bible.)

A little piece of wood once complained bitterly because its owner kept whittling away at it, cutting it, and filling it with holes, but the one who was cutting it so remorselessly paid no attention to its complaining. He was making a flute out of that piece of ebony, and he was too wise to desist from doing so, even though the wood complained bitterly. He seemed to say, "Little piece of wood, without these holes and all this cutting, you would be a black stick forever—just a useless piece of ebony. What I am doing now may make you think I am destroying you, but instead, I will change you into a flute, and your sweet music will charm the souls of men and comfort many a sorrowing heart. My cutting you is the making of you, for only thus can you be a blessing in the world."[1]

I wonder what beautiful music the Lord wants to play through you to the world around you. Will you surrender yourself to Him? Will you dare to plumb the depths of God's Word? Will you pay the price in time and energy and cultivate time alone with God? Will you adjust your life to what the Holy Spirit shows you in God's Word? Will you pray His Word and respond to Him in prayer? Then watch as He transforms you, making you like Jesus Christ. And then revel in the great adventure of knowing God and making Him known to those around you.

A.W. Tozer says that a disciple is one who is facing one direction only, has stopped looking back, and has no further plans of his own. May the prayer of Betty Scott Stam be yours today: "Lord, I give up all my own plans and purposes, all my own desires and hopes, and accept Thy will for my life. I give myself, my time, my all utterly to Thee to be Thine forever. Fill me and seal me with Thy Holy Spirit. Use me as Thou wilt, send me where Thou wilt, work out Thy whole will in my life at any cost, now and forever."

My Response

DATE:

KEY VERSE: "Don't copy the behavior and customs of this world, but let God transform you into a new person by changing the way you think. Then you will know what God wants you to do" (Romans 12:2 NLT).

FOR FURTHER THOUGHT: How has knowing God transformed you from the inside out? In what ways have you surrendered to His will in your own life? What verse in the Bible can you pray today that will help you believe Him for something according to His will in your life? Write your prayer as a response to Him today.

MY RESPONSE:

Day Twenty-Four

QUIET TIME—
WEEK FOUR:
EXPERIENCING
THE ROMANCE

PREPARE YOUR HEART

George Mueller lived in England in the 1800s and at a young age attended a London seminary where he learned how to meditate on the Word of God. He was filled with a desire to depend totally on the Lord regardless of the nature of his need. The passion of his soul was to know the secrets of prevailing with God and with man. Early in his life, he read the biography of George Whitefield, and two practices stood out to him: prayer and the habit of reading the Bible on his knees. George Mueller began to read the Word of God on his knees and spend hours in meditation and prayer over a single psalm or chapter in the Bible.

A.T. Pierson, in his biography *George Mueller of Bristol,* says this: "It was habits of life such as these, and not impulsive feelings and transient frames, that made this man of God what he was and strengthened him to lift up his hands in God's name, and follow hard after Him and in Him rejoice."[1] God used George Mueller in a powerful way. Mueller taught 121,000 students; distributed 300,000 Bibles, 1.5 million New Testaments, and 11 million tracts; and built five orphanages that daily fed 2100 orphans. Charles Dickens wrote about orphans at the same time that Mueller was feeding them. The secret: the Bible in Mueller's life. He made a rule to never begin work until he had a good season with God. He read the Bible through more than a hundred times, half of the time on his knees.

As you begin your time with the Lord, think about George Mueller's conviction to be in the Bible and prayer before ever beginning the work of the day. Meditate on David's words in Psalm 5 as a preparation of heart. Then ask God to speak to you from His Word.

READ AND STUDY GOD'S WORD

David, the shepherd who became king of God's people, was a man after God's own heart. One of the great hallmarks of David's life was his vibrant relationship with the Lord. Read 1 Samuel 23:1-14 and write out everything you notice about David's relationship with God.

As you looked at David's relationship with God, what did you notice about their conversation? What happened when David inquired of the Lord? How important were God's words to David?

Look at the following verses and record what you learn about prayer. Be sure to personalize your insights. For example, "I am going to ask and it will be given to me."

Matthew 7:7

1 John 3:18-24

1 John 5:14-15

One way to know if you are praying according to the will of God as seen in 1 John 5:14-15 is to pray to God using His Word as a guide. Pray the following prayers for yourself and someone else in your life today:

Ephesians 3:14-21

Colossians 1:9-12

ADORE GOD IN PRAYER

You have seen in George Mueller's life the great value of praying God's Word. Turn to Psalm 31 and use these words (written by David, the man after God's own heart) to talk with God today.

YIELD YOURSELF TO GOD

Here then we have a threefold witness to the secret of true prosperity and unmingled blessing: devout meditation and reflection upon the Scriptures, which are at once a book of life, a river of life, and a mirror of self—fitted to convey the will of God, the life of God, and the transforming power of God. That believer makes a fatal mistake who for any cause neglects the prayerful study of the word of God. To read God's holy book, by it search one's self, and turn it into prayer and so into holy living is the one great secret of growth in grace and godliness. The worker for God must first be a worker with God; he must have power with God and must prevail with Him in prayer, if he is to have power with men and prevail with men in preaching or in any form of witnessing and serving. At all costs let us make sure of that highest preparation for our work—the preparation of our own souls; and for this we must take time to be alone with His word and His Spirit, that we may truly meet God, and understand His will and the revelation of Himself.

If we unlock the secrets of the life George Mueller lived and the work he did, this is the very key to the whole mystery, and with that key any believer can unlock the doors to a prosperous growth in grace and power in service. God's word is HIS WORD—the expression of His thought, the revealing of His mind and heart. The supreme end of life is to know God and make Him known; and how is this possible if we neglect the very means He has chosen for conveying to us that knowledge! Even Christ, the Living Word, is to be found enshrined in the written word. Our knowledge of Christ is dependent upon our acquaintance with the Holy Scriptures, which are the reflection of His character and glory—the firmament across the expanse of which He moves as the Sun of righteousness.[2]

ARTHUR T. PIERSON
GEORGE MUELLER OF BRISTOL

ENJOY HIS PRESENCE

Think about the relationship of prayer to the Bible. Will you take encouragement from George Mueller today and begin to read the Word of God on your knees? Close by writing a prayer to the Lord, expressing all that is on your heart.

Rest in His Love

"This is the confidence which we have before Him, that, if we ask anything according to His will, He hears us. And if we know that He hears us in whatever we ask, we know that we have the requests which we have asked from Him" (1 John 5:14-15).

Notes — Week Four

ENJOY THE ROMANCE

Days 25-30

Day Twenty-Five

LIFE IN THE WORD

We look not at the things which are seen,
but at the things which are not seen, for
the things which are seen are temporal, but
the things which are not seen are eternal.

2 CORINTHIANS 4:18

What you look at determines how you see. And how you see determines how you live. Paul told the church at Corinth, "We look not at the things which are seen, but at the things which are not seen, for the things which are seen are temporal, but the things which are not seen are eternal" (2 Corinthians 4:18). This is the biblical description of the eternal perspective; the ability to see all of life from God's point of view and have what you see affect how you live in the present. One of the great results of an eternal perspective is the ability to not lose heart in difficult trials and circumstances. The eternal perspective you gain by looking into the mirror of the Bible will determine the course and character of your life.

Darlene and Russell Deibler were married on August 18, 1937. Within the first year of their marriage, they arrived as missionaries in

Dutch New Guinea (today's West Papua). On December 8, 1941, the Japanese invaded Pearl Harbor. One by one, West Indies islands fell, and it was only a matter of time for New Guinea. One day Darlene heard a truck approach the missionary house and stop. An army officer entered the house and declared he was taking the men. Darlene rushed to get Russell's Bible and other things she thought he would need and stuffed them into a pillowcase. But she couldn't find Russell. She dashed out into the yard and saw that he was already in the back of the truck with the other POWs. She ran over to the truck, handed Russell the pillowcase, and looked into the face that had become so dear to her, her husband of only five years. Refusing to allow the soldiers to see her cry, she silently thought to herself how they had not even let her say goodbye. Russell leaned over the tailgate and very quietly said, "Remember one thing, dear. God said He would never leave or forsake us." Those were the last words she heard from her dear husband, for she never saw him again.

When all your earthly hopes have dimmed, what is going to carry you through and enable you to endure? When dreams become disappointment and this life seems to hold no future, what is going to give you hope? One thing only: an eternal perspective. You need God's eternal perspective, seen in the mirror of the Bible, every single day of your life.

An eternal perspective enabled Darlene to sing hymns in a dark, damp jail cell as she suffered cruel deprivation and torture. An eternal perspective enabled Corrie ten Boom to minister to hundreds of women in the concentration camp at Ravensbruck. An eternal perspective gave Esther Ahn Kim the courage to stand tall in a crowd as all others bowed to a pagan shrine. It was an eternal perspective that gave John Bunyan the insight to write the classic *Pilgrim's Progress* from a prison cell. An eternal perspective will enable you to endure when you feel as though you cannot go on.

We can look at life two ways. First, we can look at what is seen, what is temporal. This is man's view of feelings and circumstances, seen and experienced with the physical eye. If this is all a person sees, the result is a tendency to lose heart. Paul says in 1 Corinthians 15:19 that "if we have hoped in Christ in this life only, we are of all men most to be pitied."

The second way of looking at life is to look at what is not seen, at what is eternal. This is God's point of view—the eternal perspective. What you see cannot be seen with physical eyes because it's invisible, but it's nevertheless true and real. In fact, it is more true than what can be seen with the physical eye. The result of an eternal perspective is a hope, a great expectation that anchors the soul and is independent of outside events.

Paul says in Romans 8:24-25, "For in hope we have been saved, but hope that is seen is not hope; for who hopes for what he already sees? But if we hope for what we do not see, with perseverance we wait eagerly for it." The eternal perspective is the truth, the reality in any situation. It is the ability to see your circumstances through God's eyes. Where can you find God's point of view? Only one place—the Bible, God's Word. When you go to the Bible, you gain God's perspective for your situation.

What do you need in order to gain the eternal perspective?

- *You must be a Christian.* To become a Christian involves praying to Jesus and asking Him to come into your life. Christians are indwelt by the Holy Spirit. You must be spiritual in order to understand spiritual things. Spiritual things are spiritually discerned (see 1 Corinthians 2:6-16).

- *You must acknowledge your present situation in life.* You cannot gain a proper perspective if you deny your circumstances. Denial shortcuts your ability to see God's view. Truth will make you free (see John 8:32).

- *You must discover God's point of view in His Word.* Find God's promises related to your situation in life (see 2 Peter 1:4). For example, if you don't feel loved, look up every verse you can find in the Bible on love. If you are suffering, look up promises related to trials. Review God's eternal promises as they relate to your life in the future with Him—such as promises about heaven, eternity, your future state, and your future with the Lord Jesus.

- *You must take God at His Word.* Act according to the eternal perspective you have seen in God's Word. This means you walk by faith, not by sight (see 2 Corinthians 5:7). Faith is a choice, a decision, not a feeling. Believe God's perspective is absolutely true and then act on it. In your journey of knowing and loving the Bible, it is imperative that you understand how to gain the eternal perspective. Why? Because then you know what to do with the Word once you discover truth in it. You must act on it in every situation of life.

I will never forget when God began to bring an eternal perspective into focus for me. Have you ever had certain experiences with the Lord that seem to be etched into your mind and heart, never to be forgotten? It was the summer between my junior and senior year in college. I had applied to go to a Campus Crusade for Christ summer project in San Diego, but I received a rejection letter in the mail informing me that it was already filled. I was so disappointed. However, our disappointments are often God's appointments. Soon after, I received a phone call asking if I would be interested in joining the Honolulu summer project. I asked, "You mean…as in Honolulu, Hawaii?"

Summer projects are designed so that students can work part-time and learn how to share their faith during evenings and weekends. I was told I would have to trust God for the airfare and a job when I got to Hawaii. God raised the money very quickly for the airfare, and all that was left was getting a job once I got to Hawaii. I thought that would be no problem because I had good job experience as a sales clerk in a department store. In addition, I could type really fast. So I thought certainly I would be able to find some kind of work. Well, I got to Hawaii and could not find a job anywhere. No one was even remotely interested in me. So there I was, without a job in a strange place. I believed that God was going to do great things and that He had a job picked out especially for me. I asked everyone I met if they knew where I could get a job.

At first, I was positive and hopeful. But after some time, and after watching all the other students get jobs, I began to get discouraged. Finally, I began to get desperate. One day, I took a bus to the middle of downtown Honolulu and filled out an application at an employment agency, thinking maybe they could find me a job. They said they didn't have anything. I walked out of that building one of the saddest people you've ever seen. I was in the middle of nowhere, walking in an alley under a freeway, in a place where I didn't know anyone, with no job and no hope of ever getting a job. I had a splitting headache and started crying. Suddenly, I stopped. It was as though the large hand of God stopped me. I had an overwhelming sense that the Lord wanted to get across some point with me, that He was teaching me something very crucial to my walk with Him—a life-changing truth.

I began thinking about what I had been recently reading in Hebrews 11. I read about Abraham and how he had left his own country to go to a strange place because God wanted him to. I learned that he had gone out without knowing where he was going and had lived as an alien in a foreign land. Then I said out loud, "Lord, this is the way it is going to be for the rest of my life, isn't it? I am a stranger and an alien on planet earth. You are going to take me to all kinds of places. Many times it will be uncomfortable. And I can never call any place truly home, because my real home is with you. I will be home with you very soon in light of eternity. Life on earth is for a brief moment compared to eternity. Lord, even though everything will always change, You never change, and You will be with me wherever I go. Thank You, Lord."

Then I dried my eyes. I smiled with the Lord and even started laughing. I had learned an incredible truth. I had begun to take on an eternal perspective. I had realized I was on earth for the Lord, not for myself. Everything was to be seen in light of my eternal life with Christ, and that included being willing to accomplish His purposes in strange places. It meant at times I would feel like an alien and a stranger, out of place and uncomfortable. My time on earth would be brief compared to eternity. I made a decision at that moment. I decided that for the rest of my life I wanted to accomplish the Lord's purposes.

Very soon after that experience I was walking to the bus stop. I saw a young man walking toward the bus and felt I should ask him about a job. I ran up to him and told him I was looking for a summer job. He said he was just hired yesterday, and maybe I could get a job there too. When I showed up to apply for the job, a big Hawaiian woman was behind the counter. I could hear one of my favorite songs, "My Tribute," on the radio. I asked the lady at the counter why she was smiling. She said, "Because I have Jesus Christ in my life." I knew that was God's job for me. I worked in a hotel lobby selling pineapples, papayas, and coconuts to all the tourists. And I got to share with many of my customers how to have a relationship with Jesus Christ. A lot of them prayed to receive Christ with me. I would put up my little sign that said BE RIGHT BACK, and we would go to the side of the lobby and pray together. It was the most exciting summer of my life. I learned something very important that summer. I learned that God wants to do extraordinary things through ordinary, unimportant, weak people. And I learned that God wants me to have an eternal perspective.

How are you doing in having an eternal perspective about things? When you gain an eternal perspective, you will see the power of God's Word at work in your life. You learn to walk and live by faith in His Word. Do you operate according to an eternal perspective? If you are having a problem maintaining an eternal perspective, check for a breakdown in one of the steps I mentioned. Are you acknowledging your present situation? Where do you look for God's perspective, the Word or the world? Are you familiar with God's promises and your future with Him? Are you obedient to the perspective that God is giving you? Are you walking by faith, taking God at His word? And most importantly, are you a Christian? Have you received Jesus Christ into your life? This is a "once and for all" decision described in John 3:16, "God so loved the world, that He gave His only begotten Son, that whoever believes in Him will not perish, but have eternal life."

When you look into the mirror of God's Word, always look for the promises of God. A promise is something God says He will do. God's promises are keys that unlock the door to God's eternal perspective. God wants you to find His promises, embrace them, trust them, and live them out in your life. Whenever you find a promise from God, write it in your journal and memorize it so you can make it your own.

All the great men and women of God have had a firm grasp of God's perspective and have acted according to what they saw in the Bible. That's why Jim Elliot was able to say: "He is no fool who gives up what he cannot keep to gain what he cannot lose."[1] Darlene Deibler Rose, the woman who lost her husband and who eventually herself was imprisoned and tortured in World War II, speaks of an old Roman coin on which is found the picture of an ox. The ox is facing two things: an altar and a plow. The inscription reads, "Ready for either." Some may be called upon to make the supreme sacrifice on the altar of martyrdom.

Most of us will be called upon to put our hands to the plow of service for the Master, never looking back, and bearing the cost of following Him until He calls us home. The only way you will be able to do it is by knowing and loving the Bible and gaining an eternal perspective. Those who have gone before you—Moses, Abraham, Isaiah, David, Paul, Martin Luther, John Wesley, and of course, Jesus, encourage you to know that it is worth it all.

My Response

DATE:

KEY VERSE: "We look not at the things which are seen, but at the things which are not seen; for the things which are seen are temporal, but the things which are not seen are eternal" (2 Corinthians 4:18).

FOR FURTHER THOUGHT: Describe in your own words what it means to have an eternal perspective. Why is the Bible so important when seeking God's eternal perspective? In what way do you need His eternal perspective today?

MY RESPONSE:

THE LIFE OF PRAYER

Pray without ceasing.

1 THESSALONIANS 5:17

U nceasing prayer characterizes your life when you live with God in His Word. Paul exhorts the church at Thessalonica to "pray without ceasing" (1 Thessalonians 5:17). Clement of Alexandria defined prayer as "keeping company with God." This unceasing prayer begins as you open the pages of the Bible and meet with God there. It increases in intensity as you walk with God, traversing with Him across the landscape of the Bible. It becomes part of your nature as you build a life with the Lord, living daily with Him in His Word. And it is one of the great hallmarks of those who enjoy the romance of God and His Word.

Alice Smith describes how impressed she was the first time she ever met Corrie ten Boom. When Corrie ten Boom entered the room, Alice had a profound sense of spiritual goodness, kindness, and love emanating from her. Corrie would sit and talk about spiritual things and then, in the middle of her conversation with people in the room, she would look up and say "Yes, Lord," or "I see, Lord," or "Thank You, Lord." Corrie was so aware of the Lord's constant presence with her that including Him in the conversation was completely natural. In fact, Corrie would probably have felt unkind and antisocial had she not acknowledged her dear Lord in their midst.

That is what unceasing prayer is all about. It means keeping company with God all the time. There is no time He is not with you. To not converse with Him would be impolite. Corrie ten Boom used to say, "Is prayer your steering wheel or is it your spare tire?" This is the great challenge for you and for me. We do well to look forward to high planes of life, great vistas in our spiritual walk with God that we have not yet reached. We have more of God to discover. We will have deeper conversations with Him. He wants to tell us secrets from His Word that we do not yet comprehend.

When we pray unceasingly, we are conscious of God and include Him in every detail of our lives. Our ability to do this and our practice of unceasing prayer increases as we know and love the Bible more and more. Unceasing prayer set David, the man after God's own heart, apart from all others. He sat in the presence of the Lord. He inquired of the Lord before making decisions.

Prayer is not a formula or a magic pill to take in order to make things happen in your life. Prayer is an integral part of your relationship with God in His Word. As you read the Bible, your natural response before, during, and after your time in God's Word is prayer. Prayer is talking with God. It is pouring your soul out to God. It is companionship with God. The Bible does not come to you in a vacuum but in a relationship with God. Within the context of this relationship, God speaks to you in His Word. How can you remain silent? You cannot help but respond to what God says to you. Prayer is natural in the conversation of the Word. In the Word, God says many things. He encourages you. He comforts you. Sometimes He challenges you. He shows you a larger view of Himself and His ways. He may point out to you something you did wrong. This is the conviction of the Holy Spirit. And He may ask for a decision from you. Whatever He says requires a response in you. And you communicate that response in prayer. It may begin with silent reverence. It may be praise. It may be thanksgiving. It may be confession. It may be intercession on behalf of another as you see the great promises of God. It may be commitment. It may be affirmation of truth. God's words in the Bible prompt you to pray. And your response in prayer will include words of trust, affirmation of spiritual truth, confession and repentance of sin, a statement of belief in what God says, a decision to change, a yielding to God's ways, and commitments to love others and even share the Word with others.

The Bible teaches you how to say these things to God in a powerful way. The Bible orders your prayers. It teaches you what to pray and how to pray. It gives you more to say than you could ever dream up on your own. In fact, the Bible will change your prayers. It lifts your prayers to new heights.

Paul encouraged the Philippians, a church that was suffering, with these words: "Don't worry about anything; instead, pray about everything. Tell God what you need, and thank him for all that he has done. If you do this, you will experience God's peace, which is far more wonderful than the human mind can understand. His peace will guard your hearts and minds as you live in Christ Jesus" (Philippians 4:6-7 NLT). When you live a life of prayer in fellowship with your Lord, you will experience a peace that is independent of feelings or circumstances. This is one of the great benefits of your romance with God and His Word. It is that very quality of God's peace in you that will speak to a lost and hurting world in the midst of great crisis and trauma. God's peace will enable you to minister to hearts that are weary and in need of God's touch. Doors will open in ministry, and opportunities will become available to you. It all begins with the divine romance with God and His Word and with living a life of unceasing prayer throughout the day.

My Response

DATE:

KEY VERSE: "Pray without ceasing" (1 Thessalonians 5:17).

FOR FURTHER THOUGHT: Describe in your own words what it means to pray without ceasing. How does the Bible help you pray more? What would you like to talk with God about today? Will you take some time now to talk with Him?

MY RESPONSE:

MINISTRY: JESUS CHRIST IN ACTION

*But thanks be to God, who always leads
us in triumph in Christ, and manifests
through us the sweet aroma of the
knowledge of Him in every place.*

2 CORINTHIANS 2:14

Jesus wants to touch other people through you. When you live with Him in His Word, you will naturally become involved in ministry. Your ministry is part of the story of your life and the message He is writing on your heart. You will begin to sense His call to you to join Him in something He is doing in the world. The call will come from Him in His Word: "Follow Me, and I will make you fishers of men" (Matthew 4:19). You cannot help hearing His call all across the pages of the Bible. It is a call to ministry. Ministry is Jesus Christ in action. He is in the business of transforming lives, just as He has transformed your life. And He wants to use you in His business of life transformation. He is excited to live His life in and through you and to turn the world upside down. As you learn and grow in your relationship with God, you will want to share Him with others. You will be filled with a great desire to pass it on. "But thanks be to God, who always leads us in triumph in Christ, and manifests through us the sweet aroma of the knowledge of Him in every place" (2 Corinthians 2:14).

I believe this generation is desperately in need of a special breed of men and women who will count the cost and launch out on the promises of God to stand tall for Him in this world. I remember reading a little booklet many years ago entitled *Many Aspire, Few Attain.* Just the title was enough to motivate me. I knew I wanted very much to be the one who actually attained. I could not imagine a worse outcome than to have aspired in life but never to have attained. Many people in this generation think they have attained because they are doing a lot and have acquired many possessions. But what is success in God's eyes? I believe it is to know and love God and live by His Word in the strength and power of the Holy Spirit every day of your life. It does not mean that we must accomplish thousands of tasks in a day, or a month, or a year. The worst outcome in life would be to have accomplished much but not to know God intimately.

When you are intimate with God, He will give you ideas for ministry. That is how He works. Paul told the church at Corinth, "Now there are varieties of gifts, but the same Spirit. And there are varieties of ministries, and the same Lord. There are varieties of effects, but the same God who works all things in all persons" (1 Corinthians 12:4-6). God has gifted you and has a ministry in mind for you. He wants to influence certain people in a certain way through your life. Because of this, He is going to put ideas in your mind that will help you touch other peoples' lives. What are you going to do about those ideas? My suggestion is to take Him seriously, write down each idea, and begin to think about it and pray about it. If the idea will not go away, then it might be God's idea. Ask Him for wisdom and then begin mapping out a plan to see that idea become reality. Take the initiative, in the power of the Holy Spirit, and act on the ideas. Then leave the results to God.

When I was in seminary, I spent an evening working on an assignment from my New Testament professor. I had to outline the entire book of Romans. I completed my time in Romans close to midnight. I was so overwhelmed with a sense of the presence of God that I fell to my knees. The magnificence of God's plan was so apparent to me in Romans. I thought if God could do all that, He deserved my greatest surrender. I gave Him every part of myself that night. That's what happens when you come face-to-face with the Lord in His Word. He brings you to a place of surrender so He can use you in His ministry. Little did I know that He was about to give me a huge calling and responsibility.

Just prior to my seminary graduation, I was sitting in my family room having my quiet time. I was thinking about all the people who were coming to me, asking me about quiet time. Their question was always the same: Where do I begin? I thought about the statistics of those who attend church—only 45 percent ever open their Bibles outside of their time in church. All of a sudden, sitting there, I got an idea. What if I put together a notebook just like what I use in my quiet time? And what if I had a ministry that focused on teaching others how to spend quiet time with the Lord? I could even publish a newsletter on quiet time. I was so excited that when my husband came home from work, I would not let him move until I told him my idea. It was just an idea. But it was God's idea, and He made it come to life. It was a defining moment for me and it was the beginning of Quiet Time Ministries. It began with a notebook that took me a year to create. Then a newsletter. I was a young woman who was crazy enough to believe in a big God who could do anything. Someone told me once, "You be responsible for the depth of your ministry and let God be responsible for the breadth of your ministry." My responsibility was to go deep with God, to grow in my relationship with Him, and He would be responsible for how far and wide the ministry He gave me would go. Of course, I had no idea exactly how expansive the scope of Quiet Time Ministries would become.

All of this began as a simple idea I had in my quiet time with the Lord. Ministry must begin with the Lord if it is to materialize and grow in God's way. In addition, it must continue with the Lord if it is to become what He wants it to be and accomplish what He has in mind. With this in mind, I want to ask you this: Has God placed certain ideas on your heart? If so, what are you doing with them? As you know and love the Bible, He will give you ideas for ministry. That is how ministry begins. If your idea won't go away, then I challenge you to write it out in your journal and begin praying about it. Ask God to write His message on your heart. Ask Him to use all the gifts and talents He has given you so you can glorify Him. And then launch out on His promises in the strength and power of the Holy Spirit. I want to challenge you to dare to act on the ideas that God puts in your heart and mind and then give them wings to fly. Ministry really is Jesus Christ in action. As you walk with Him, He will do a great and mighty work in and through you to touch the world.

My Response

DATE:

KEY VERSE: "But thanks be to God, who always leads us in triumph in Christ, and manifests through us the sweet aroma of the knowledge of Him in every place" (2 Corinthians 2:14).

FOR FURTHER THOUGHT: How do you feel about the idea of God using you to impact the lives of those around you? Has He given you any ideas for ministry to reach out to others? If so, write out those ideas and then begin to pray about them. Perhaps God is writing a message on your heart that is going to influence the world. To God be the glory!

MY RESPONSE:

Day Twenty-Eight

HOW TO START
A REVIVAL

*If anyone believes in me, rivers of living
water will flow out from that person's heart.*

JOHN 7:38 NCV

J esus wants to start a revival in you and through you. He says, "Let anyone who is thirsty come to me and drink. If anyone believes in me, rivers of living water will flow out from that person's heart" (John 7:37-38 NCV). Personal revival comes from your time in the Bible. Personal revival as it is described in such places in the Bible as Psalm 119 is a quickening of heart and soul by God, imparting whatever is necessary to sustain one's spiritual life and enable a return to the experience of one's true purpose as ordained by God. Isaiah paints this picture of revival: "The LORD will guide you continually, watering your life when you are dry and keeping you healthy, too. You will be like a well-watered garden, like an ever-flowing spring" (Isaiah 58:11 NLT).

The church is in desperate need of revival today. In fact, a crisis is brewing in the church. It is one of the greatest challenges the church faces, and if the church does not come to grips with it, the church will literally fall apart. This crisis is the reason for complacency. It is the cause of immorality and a thousand other things that plague the church today. What is this great crisis? It is something known in theological circles as the authority for one's belief. God, through His Word, the Bible, is to be the authority for our belief. This means that we are to allow the words of the Bible to form our beliefs and convictions and to tell us what to do.

Why do I say this is now the crisis of the church? Statistics have demonstrated that over half of those who attend church never open their Bibles outside of church. Either you are in the Word or you are in the world. Either God and His Word form your beliefs and actions or the world does. No wonder the church is lackluster and often complacent. Most in the church are experiencing religion without relationship. Why? Because to many in the church, the Bible is a closed book. This is to our shame. The Bible is accessible to us. In fact, many have more than one Bible. Unfortunately, most Bibles are sitting on shelves or tables. Those of us who are leaders in the church are given the stewardship of passing on what we have learned to those around us. Why is this not happening? I am convinced it is because many have not learned it. I believe many leaders in the church have stepped away from God and His Word and are pursuing many other things. What we need is the one thing—the main thing—the Lord. This may sound like a harsh indictment, but it is meant as a strong exhortation to get back to the main thing so that we may walk intimately with our Lord, become the men and women He has designed us to be, and make an incredible and astounding difference in the world where we live. How can we be salt if we lose our savor? How can we be light if the flame goes out?

George Barna has predicted that in the next ten years America will experience either widespread spiritual revival or absolute cultural anarchy.[1] What we need is revival. God determines when He will blow the winds of His Spirit in such a way as to bring corporate revival. But corporate revival is surrounded and determined by individuals who know personal revival as a way of life. Revival depends upon the intentional response of God's people in the midst of a decadent, dark, immoral society. How will we believers act in an environment that is godless, immoral, and increasingly antagonistic to Christians? How will we respond when we fail, when we lose our jobs, when we are persecuted for our beliefs? What will we do when we are tempted to grow weary and lose heart? What will we do when God seems to be hiding His face?

We live in a society that says it's okay to believe in anything as long as it's not Jesus. Once you say you believe in Jesus, you are labeled intolerant. It's almost laughable when you think about it. One newscaster has called Christianity a harsh view in the banner of religious faith. This antagonism against Jesus Christ and those who follow him has come at the same time as an increased interest in prayer, spirituality, and the soul. Secular bookstores contain many books on help for the soul. Many of these books, however, never mention Jesus Christ or biblical truth.

This is the most dangerous of all: A belief in or tolerance of many gods is considered correct, right, and true. An exclusive belief system worshipping the one true God is considered dangerous and intolerant. Few are concerned about whether it is true or not. In Matthew 24:9-14, Jesus said that in the last days, "many will fall away," and "most people's love will grow cold."

How will we, the believers in Jesus Christ, respond in the times of trouble? How can we make a difference in what happens in America and in the world? I believe we must get back to the Bible. I think the words of God through Jeremiah are applicable today: "Thus says the LORD, 'Stand by the ways and see and ask for the ancient paths, where the good way is, and walk in it; and you will find rest for your souls'" (Jeremiah 6:16). How can we make a return to the Word of God? How can we find those ancient paths? How can you respond in such a way that you can experience personal spiritual revival and be used by God in His work in the world?

Make a decision about the Word. Resolve and commit before the Lord that His Word is going to be the authority for your belief. Let the Bible form your beliefs and convictions and tell you what to do. Give God and His Word a block of time in your life. This needs to happen on a daily basis. Write a prayer of commitment to the Lord about your decision to draw near to Him and live in His Word.

Get a good cross-reference Bible. Make certain that it is easy to read and carry, not so large that you can't take it with you and not so small that you need a magnifying glass to read it. Choose a translation such as the New American Standard Bible, the New International Version, the New King James Version, the New Living Translation, or the English Standard Version.

Choose a Bible reading plan. Decide how you are going to be in God's Word. You may want to get a one-year devotional Bible. Or choose a good Bible study. There are many available, including the books of quiet times available at Quiet Time Ministries.

Learn about quiet time and experiment with the devotional Bible studies shared in this book. The principles of quiet time and Bible study are not acquired by osmosis. These things do not come to us in some mysterious hidden way. They are learned by those who have practiced quiet time and Bible study and have experienced intimacy with God as a result. I encourage you to always be in the school of quiet time and Bible study. Read lots of books in those two areas. Your heart and mind and soul will thank you for it.

Read books and listen to messages on CDs or DVDs by those who love God and live in His Word. These men and women will challenge you in your journey with God. Choose your teachers wisely. Look at their lives. Are they spending time with God in His Word on a daily basis? If not, they have nothing to say. If God's Word is not a reality in a teacher's life, he or she must sit down until it is.

Get in a good Bible study. You may meet in a home or at a church. Make certain your Bible study actually studies the Word of God. Enjoy fellowship, but not at the expense of learning from God in His Word. Some small groups only meet to talk, and they experience no in-depth learning from the Word. Find out what your group is going to study before committing yourself to the group. Bible studies are great for accountability and learning. A good discussion of your study is incredibly valuable. It helps you articulate what God is teaching you and cements His truth in your heart and mind.

Find a good Christian bookstore to buy your books, Bibles, and other Bible study tools. Early on in my relationship with the Lord, I practically lived at the Evangelical Bible Bookstore in San Diego. John and Sandra Cully, the owners, often helped me choose good Bible study books. I pulled Bible study tools off the shelves, sat on the floor, and perused them to learn their use and function for Bible study. Get to know the people who run the store, and they will help you choose books that God can use to help you grow in your relationship with Him.

My prayer for you is that God and His Word will be the authority for your belief. The question in my heart is this: Could revival be around the corner? The psalmist in Psalm 119:50 said that the Word of God revived him. If the church, in full force, makes a return to God and His Word, perhaps God, by His Spirit, will blow His winds of revival upon His church, and the church will experience more life than ever before. Oh, how I pray this will happen in my lifetime!

Throughout history, God has supernaturally poured out His Spirit on groups of people. As I have studied these revivals, I have discovered that each large-scale revival featured a few outstanding individuals who were devoted to God and His Word and who knew revival in their own lives as a normal experience because they knew the God of revival.

Consider Jonathan Edwards and George Whitefield during the Great Awakening in the 1700s, David Brainerd among the American Indians, Charles Finney in America in the 1800s, and Evan Roberts in the Welsh Revival in 1904 and 1905. These men experienced revival in their own personal walks with the Lord. Long before George Whitefield saw revival break out under his preaching, he said he began to read Scripture on his knees, laying aside all other books and praying over every line and word. He prayed, "God, give me a deep humility, a well-guided zeal, a burning love, and a single eye...may I be little in my own eyes, and not rob my dear Master of any part of His glory." Here was a man who knew God and experienced revival in his own life. God used George Whitefield in a powerful way in one of the greatest corporate revivals.

Brian Edwards says in his book *Revival,* "Those whom God uses in leadership in revival are always men who have met with God in a powerfully personal way and have a burning passion for the glory of God and a life of holiness."

In the late 1800s Wales saw a major decline in church membership, a loss of power in the pulpits, and a deterioration of piety and devotion among the members of all the churches. A tremendous indifference plagued the Christians. Burdened by his concern about this indifference, an unknown pastor named Joseph Jenkins sought to know Christ more and began intently reading Andrew Murray's book *With Christ in the School of Prayer*. As he did, he became more and more burdened by the apathy toward God in the lives of those around him. And so, he began talking very seriously about obedience to the Holy Spirit. One morning in 1904, a meeting of the Young People's Society in his city experienced a very sincere movement of response to God as Reverend Jenkins spoke. Soon people began meeting and sharing testimonies about God working in their lives. After six months, a man named Seth Joshua arrived in the area to conduct meetings. He remarked that he had never seen such power of the Holy Spirit among people. He himself felt saturated by God, melted, and made soft as clay. Attending one of his meetings was Evan Roberts, age 26, who had been burdened to pray for revival since the age of 13. He believed the Holy Spirit had moved him to think about revival. As Seth Joshua closed one of his messages he prayed, "Lord bend us!" Evan Roberts was so moved that he walked to the front of the room and cried out, "Lord, bend me!" A wave of peace flooded his soul, and he became concerned about others. He said, "I felt ablaze with a desire to go through the length and breadth of Wales to tell of the Savior." He began conducting meetings all over Wales, spreading the fires of revival. Chapels were filled, with hundreds more people outside. Some people have said that in 1904 and 1905, all of Wales seemed like a praise meeting. Passionate prayer continued day after day, night after night for a full year. Preaching at times was out of the question as people were so moved by the desire to pour their hearts out in prayer to God. It was an exciting time. But you can see that behind it were simple people: Joseph Jenkins, Seth Joshua, and Evan Roberts. They were devoted to God and His Word, burdened for God's people, and saturated by God Himself. And many others, too many to name, were also instrumentally involved in prayer and devotion to God as part of the Welsh revival of 1904.

God is stirring believers' hearts. What if God really is searching to and fro throughout the earth that He may strongly support those whose hearts are completely His (2 Chronicles 16:9)? May you and I be devoted to God and His Word. Perhaps, as God personally revives us, He may privilege us to witness and experience a great revival in America.

John Wesley said, "Give me one hundred men who fear nothing but sin and desire nothing but God, and I will shake the world." I wonder what would happen if 100 men and women would wholeheartedly turn to the Lord and give themselves to time in God's Word? May you and I be counted as part of that group in our lifetime, and may the Lord use us as lights and salt where we live to influence the world for Christ.

Gypsy Smith was once asked how to start a revival. He answered, "Go home, lock yourself in your room, kneel down in the middle of your floor. Draw a chalk mark all around yourself and ask God to start the revival inside that chalk mark. When He has answered your prayer, the revival will be on."

My Response

DATE:

KEY VERSE: "If anyone believes in me, rivers of living water will flow out from that person's heart" (John 7:38 NCV).

FOR FURTHER THOUGHT: How will you apply what you have learned on this 30-day journey of knowing and loving the Bible? In what ways has God been reviving your own heart? What are the most important decisions those in the church need to make about the Bible? Why are your own decisions about the Word of God so important? What decision do you need to make about the Bible today?

MY RESPONSE:

Day Twenty-Nine

THE RIPPLE EFFECT

Go therefore and make disciples of all the
nations, baptizing them in the name of the
Father and the Son and the Holy Spirit.

MATTHEW 28:19

Your life is so significant to God that He wants to use you for purposes that will last forever. Jesus has given you a commission: "Go therefore and make disciples of all the nations, baptizing them in the name of the Father and the Son and the Holy Spirit" (Matthew 28:19). Jesus elaborated on this commission in Acts 1:8 (NLT): "But when the Holy Spirit has come upon you, you will receive power and will tell people about me everywhere—in Jerusalem, throughout Judea, in Samaria, and to the ends of the earth." Jesus wants to be a sweet fragrance in your life and touch the lives of thousands through many generations. What He does in and through you lasts forever.

When I was a little girl, my brother and I used to go with my mother to a little park in Phoenix. She would sit and study for her master's degree, and my brother and I would play. One of the things we loved to do was pick up rocks and throw them in the middle of a pond. We would stand there for an hour and do it again and again, fascinated by the series of ripples created by the splash. The higher the rock went into the air, the more force it created when it hit the water, and the more ripples occurred as a result.

Now is the moment for you to make decisions that will create such force that you will become part of God's ripple effect in history. Now is the defining moment. All of us have had defining moments in our lives. These are the moments when we make a move in a direction, we step up to the plate, and we resolve to do something we know is right. Defining moments shape the course of our lives.

You have had the opportunity to read about a very special kind of life. It's the kind of life that stands out in a crowd. It is the life of romancing the Lord in His Word and being ushered into intimate fellowship with God. What will you do with what you have learned? I want to challenge you to make a decision to spend time with God in His Word every day. I want you to make a decision of *sola scriptura;* that God in His Word will be the sole authority for your belief. It is the decision that only God's Word has the right to command your beliefs and actions. Decisions like these will have many ramifications in your life. You choose to live by God's Word instead of feelings or circumstances. You come to know God's thoughts and ways because you are in the Bible every day. When you offer advice, you know the Bible well enough to take others to significant verses that are relevant to their situation. You stand on God's Word when you are tempted to give up. When you make mistakes or fall into sin, you run to God, confess your sin, and keep walking with Him.

What will help you embark on this romance of knowing and loving the Bible? Once you make this commitment, establish a life goal and a life verse. Ask God to give you an overall goal that is big enough to capture your heart for a lifetime. Ask Him to give you a verse in the Bible that will be your life verse. You can formulate your goal from this verse. The Lord will bring you back to that verse time and time again. It will be the one that you cannot seem to get out of your mind. And then, each year ask the Lord to give you a word and a verse for the year (see days 2 and 22). Paul says to "run in such a way that you may win" (1 Corinthians 9:24). Ordering your life by Scripture enables you to run in God's direction in life and become the man or woman He wants you to be. And then, read the Bible every day, experiment with devotional Bible study, get some new Bible study tools, go deep with God, pray the Word, and live the Word in your life. Resolve to know God and His Word better than you know any other thing. Then the ripple effect of your life is on.

What kind of difference can your life make? Many years ago a Sunday school teacher named Edward Kimball learned that he was going to die. He knew he had little time left to live, so he set out to lead all of his Sunday school students to the Lord. He led one to the Lord in the back room of a store. That student's name was D.L. Moody.

Of course, D.L. Moody went on to become a great evangelist. One day he was preaching in the British Isles, and a teacher was moved by his message. She went to her class and shared Moody's testimony with her students. Then she told her preacher that every one of her students had given their lives to the Lord. That preacher's name was F.B. Meyer.

That report by the teacher moved F.B. Meyer to realize what it meant to be brokenhearted over sin and point out the great need to lead others to Christ. F.B. Meyer came to America and preached at Moody's school in Northfield, Massachusetts. During his message he gave a heartfelt challenge: "If you're not willing to give up everything for Christ, are you willing to be made willing?"

That remark moved the heart of a young preacher named J. Wilbur Chapman. He became a great evangelist during his time. When he returned to the pastorate, he turned over his ministry to the YMCA clerk who had been his advance man. His name was Billy Sunday.

Billy Sunday conducted a revival meeting in Charlotte, North Carolina. Out of that meeting a group of laymen formed a permanent organization to continue sharing the message of Christ in their city.

Eight years later, in 1932, that group of men brought an evangelist named Mordecai Ham to their area to conduct citywide evangelistic meetings. One evening during one of the meetings, a tall, lanky 16-year-old stepped out of the choir and gave his life to Jesus Christ. His name was Billy Graham. And everyone knows the impact Billy Graham has had. It's the ripple effect.

God doesn't call everyone to be a Billy Graham. But I wonder what dreams God has in mind for you that are just waiting for your decision to draw near to Him in His Word? As you daily spend time with Him in His Word and live in fellowship with Him, He will bring those dreams to life.

My challenge to you is this: Make this the defining moment when you resolve to be what you have never been, do what you have never done, and dream what you have never dreamed. May the Lord bless you as you continue on in the great adventure of knowing Him!

My Response

DATE:

KEY VERSE: "Go therefore and make disciples of all the nations, baptizing them in the name of the Father and the Son and the Holy Spirit" (Matthew 28:19).

FOR FURTHER THOUGHT: How do you feel about the possibility of a ripple effect as a result of your life? Will you believe God to do a mighty work in and through you? Ask Him to give you a life goal and a life verse. And then, watch and see the great and amazing things the Lord does in your life as you walk and live, day by day, with Him.

MY RESPONSE:

Day Thirty

QUIET TIME—
WEEK FIVE:
ENJOYING THE
ROMANCE

*I will lift up my eyes to the mountains; from
where shall my help come? My help comes
from the LORD, who made heaven and earth.*

PSALM 121:1-2

PREPARE YOUR HEART

You have spent the last 29 days thinking about how you can know and love the Bible and experience God in His Word. Some rare souls will pay the price in time and energy to open the pages of God's Word, draw near to God, and actually touch the hem of His garments. You can always recognize the ones who have drawn near. They have a light in their eyes and a determination that comes from being in the presence of the King of kings and Lord of lords. They have heard the invitation to "be still, and know that I am God." And they have answered in the crucible of the ordinary day, where they have stepped away from the crowd and lived in many places of the Bible that others have not known. They have taken the time to learn how to get the nuggets of gold that God is offering to all. And they have engaged in a great adventure, for God has used them to move and change the world. Spurgeon knew that life. Moody knew it. Amy Carmichael knew it. And you can know it too. Life is either one of waste or worth. You can invest in what lasts forever. Will you resolve to take the time each day to breathe the air of heaven and walk, hand in hand, with your Lord through life? If the answer is yes, then get ready for the adventure. You will traverse lots of hills and valleys, but the view is breathtaking.

As you begin your quiet time today, turn to Psalm 121 and meditate on the words. Write your favorite phrase from this psalm in the space provided. Then write a prayer, asking the Lord to speak to you.

READ AND STUDY GOD'S WORD

Think about how we can live in the present and yet touch eternity. Look at the following verses and record what you learn.

Psalm 119:105

1 Corinthians 13:12

2 Corinthians 3:18

2 Corinthians 4:18

Colossians 3:1-4

2 Peter 1:19-21

As you think about these verses, how does God's Word help you see and know and understand eternal things?

ADORE GOD IN PRAYER

> My Lord, teach me how to walk through the ways of time and yet breathe the air of eternity. May the breezes from the hills of God blow down the vale, and in their inspiration may I find my strength!
>
> JOHN HENRY JOWETT
> *Yet Another Day*

YIELD YOURSELF TO GOD

> There should be a hill country in every life, some great up-towering peaks which dominate the common plain. There should be an upland district, where springs are born, and where rivers of inspiration have their birth. "I will lift up mine eyes unto the hills." The soul that knows no hills is sure to be oppressed with the monotony of the road. The inspiration to do little things comes from the presence of big things. It is amazing what dull trifles we can get through when a radiant love is near. A noble companionship glorifies the dingiest road. And what if that Companion be God?

Then surely, the common round and daily task have a light thrown upon them from the beauty of His countenance.

JOHN HENRY JOWETT
"The Hill Country of the Soul," *My Daily Meditation*

ENJOY HIS PRESENCE

Have you discovered the radiant love of God shining from His Word? Have you lifted your eyes and traveled to the hill country of the soul by opening the pages of your Bible day by day? If so, you will enjoy that noble companionship of your Lord that will glorify the dingiest road and dominate the landscape of your life. Your fellowship with God will bring light to every darkness and meaning to every detail of the day. God bless you as you continue on in this great adventure of knowing Him. Turn to the day 1 response and read the letter you wrote to the Lord. What has been the result of these last 30 days as you have thought about knowing and loving the Bible? How have they changed your own relationship with God and His Word? How will this time you have spent, this investment in your relationship with the Lord, make a difference in what you do with His Word? Close your time today by writing a prayer of thanksgiving and praise to God, expressing all that is on your heart.

REST IN HIS LOVE

"These things I have spoken to you so that My joy may be in you, and that your joy may be made full (John 15:11)."

Notes — Week Five

APPENDIXES

DISCUSSION QUESTIONS

These questions are for people who share this 30-day journey together. *Knowing and Loving the Bible* is a great tool for talking together about the Bible. It also provides for a great 30-day spiritual growth campaign experience. God bless you in your great adventure of knowing God.

INTRODUCTION

Use the Introduction week to meet those in your group, hand out the book *Knowing and Loving the Bible* to each participant, familiarize everyone with the topic of knowing and loving the Bible, and play the introduction message (if you are using the weekly DVD messages for *Knowing and Loving the Bible*). A good question to begin your group time is, what brought you to this 30-day journey? How did you hear about it? Allow everyone to share. Then pass out the books and explain how each week is organized according to six days with a quiet time on the sixth day. Show your group all the information in the appendixes. Tell them about the websites www.lovingthebible.com and www.quiettime.org and the message boards at www.quiettimecafe.com, where they may share insights online with others. Then describe the weekly class organization, including your group discussion followed by a DVD message (if you are using the weekly DVD messages for *Knowing and Loving the Bible*). You may want to use a sign-up sheet for snacks. Close in prayer.

WEEK ONE: THE DIVINE ROMANCE

DAY 1: The Invitation to the Divine Romance

1. Begin your time together in prayer. Then ask your group to describe their experience of spending daily time thinking about the Word of God.

2. After reading through all the days in this first week, how would you describe the divine romance? What does that mean?

3. What was your favorite statement in day 1? What challenged you? What encouraged you?

4. Describe what it means to have face-to-face fellowship with God.

5. Pages 15–16 provide reasons to know and love the Bible. Why do you want to know and love the Bible? What is your greatest motivation?

DAY 2: The Story of Your Life

1. This day begins with this statement: "God wants to tell a story to the world through you." Describe your own adventure with the Word of God to this point. What has been your journey with the Bible, and how has it impacted your relationship with the Lord?

2. If you had time to make a memorial to the Lord, what did you learn about the story of your own life? How would you describe the message God is writing on your heart these days?

3. Did you ask God for a word and verse for the year? If so, what is your word and verse for the year?

4. What encouraged you the most from day 2?

5. You might point out the importance of the prayer to receive Christ in day 2. Let your group know that anyone who prayed that prayer for the first time now has forgiveness of sins, eternal life, and the beginning of the great adventure of knowing God.

DAY 3: Why I Love the Bible

1. What fact about the Bible meant the most to you from day 3?

2. What does the Bible mean to you at this time in your life?

DAY 4: The Secret Garden of God's Word

1. How is God's Word like a secret garden?

2. In day 4 we discussed how we come to the garden of God's Word in the context of a quiet time. What helped you the most in developing a quiet time with the Lord?

3. What was your favorite part of the P.R.A.Y.E.R. Quiet Time Plan?

4. What part of the P.R.A.Y.E.R. Quiet Time Plan do you feel you need to focus on at this time in your life?

DAY 5: The Treasure of God's Word

1. On day 5 you read about how God's Word is a treasure. Why is it such a treasure?

2. What was the most important truth you learned about the Bible?

3. How did the lives of William Tyndale and John Wycliffe impact you?

4. How is the Bible being attacked today in our culture? How can we make a difference in our generation as Tyndale and Wycliffe did in their generation?

DAY 6: The Divine Romance Quiet Time

1. We spent time this week reading about the Bible, and then on day 6 we had the opportunity to actually spend some time in the Bible. What did you learn from doing the quiet time? What was your most important insight from the quiet time?

2. What meant the most to you from the life of Martin Luther?

3. What meant the most to you from the life of Josiah?

4. What quote, verse, or insight encouraged you the most this week?

WEEK TWO: EMBRACE THE ROMANCE

DAY 7: The Mirror of God's Word

1. Introduce today's discussion by doing a quick review of what you discussed last week. This will be of special benefit to those who are just joining your group. You might review by sharing that knowing and loving the Bible is a divine romance as we come face-to-face with God Himself. You might share that our relationship with God can be traced to our time with Him in His Word. Share that the Word is like a garden, and it is also like a mirror. Then, we introduced the P.R.A.Y.E.R. Quiet Time Plan.

2. God's Word is like a mirror. What kinds of things do you see when you look in the mirror of God's Word?

3. How will the Bible enable you to be able to say with James Cash Penney, "My sight is gone, but my vision is better than ever"? What did he mean by that statement?

DAY 8: The Truth About Truth

1. In day 8 we talked about the great value of truth. Why is truth important?

2. What did you learn about truth that was meaningful to you?

3. Why is the Bible significant in relation to the truth?

4. What was your favorite quote in this day of reading?

DAY 9: It Really Is True!

1. In day 9 you had the opportunity to look at specific evidence to support the truth of the Bible. How does archaeological evidence help support your faith?

2. What was your favorite archaeological discovery?

DAY 10: The Holy Spirit and the Word

1. In day 10 you looked at the third Person of the triune God, the Holy Spirit. What relationship does the Holy Spirit have to the Bible?

2. What does the Holy Spirit do in our lives?

3. How will the Holy Spirit help you to know and love the Bible?

DAY 11: The Ground of Your Heart

1. In day 11 you thought about different responses to the Bible. What makes the difference is the ground of one's heart. What difference does the Bible make in the heart?

2. "It is not what you do in the Word but what the Word does in you." Share what that means.

3. You learned many ways the Word can have maximum impact on your heart. What way meant the most to you? What way is most difficult for you and why?

4. What will it take for the Word to soften the ground of your heart and be fruitful in your life?

DAY 12: Embracing the Romance Quiet Time

1. In your quiet time this week, what meant the most to you from the example of D.L. Moody?

2. What did you learn about the Word of God in the verses from Psalm 119 in Read and Study God's Word?

3. What was your most important insight in the quiet time?

4. How did this week's reading influence your life? What was your favorite quote, thought, or verse? What have you thought about most this week as you have engaged in this 30-day journey of knowing and loving the Bible?

WEEK THREE: EXPLORE THE ROMANCE

DAY 13: Journey Through the Bible

1. In the last two weeks we have been talking about developing a relationship with God and growing in our knowledge and love of the Bible. We have looked at the beauty of the Bible, its truth, its treasure, and how it impacts the heart. As we begin today, what is the most important thing you've learned so far in this 30-day journey?

2. In day 13 you were encouraged to read through the Bible in a year. What is the value of reading through the Bible?

3. Do you currently have a Bible reading plan, and if so, what is your current plan?

DAY 14: Discovering Secrets in the Word

1. In day 14 we read about adding devotional Bible study to quiet time. Have you ever been confused about the relationship of Bible study and quiet time, and if so, how did this day of reading help you?

2. How would you describe devotional Bible study as you learned in day 14?

3. How will digging deeper in God's Word make a difference in your life?

4. What secrets has God shown you in the Bible?

DAY 15: Engaging in the Romance

1. If you love God, why will you want to study the Bible?

2. What did you learn that will help you in your approach to the Bible?

3. Why is it important to personalize Scripture?

4. Why is it important to apply what we learn in God's Word to our lives?

5. What was the most important idea you learned about devotional Bible study?

Day 16: Surprised by the Bible

1. In day 16 you looked at two ways to dig deeper in the Word of God: observation study and translation study. What was the most important idea you gained from your reading? (As a leader, make certain those in your group have discovered the detailed steps for these studies in appendix 3.)

2. What is your favorite passage of Scripture in the Bible and why?

3. What is your favorite translation of the Bible?

Day 17: Encouraged by the Bible

1. Today you looked at verse study, word study, and reference or topical study. What was the most important idea you learned that you can implement in your own quiet time?

2. Did you read about a Bible study tool that intrigues you?

3. What is your favorite word in the Bible?

4. What is your favorite verse in the Bible?

Day 18: Exploring the Romance Quiet Time

1. In day 18, what meant the most to you from the quiet time?

2. What did you learn from the life of G. Campbell Morgan?

3. What is the most important truth you learned about the Word of God?

4. Did you have a favorite quote, verse, or insight from your quiet time?

5. What was the most important idea or truth you learned from your time thinking about knowing and loving the Bible this week?

WEEK FOUR: EXPERIENCE THE ROMANCE

DAY 19: Transformed by the Bible

1. For four weeks we have been looking at the Bible and what it will take to come into face-to-face fellowship with God in His Word. We have seen the beauty of God's Word, its impact on our hearts, and ways to devotionally study it in our quiet time. This week we looked at more ways to dig deeper and what happens when we do draw near to God in His Word.

   As you spent this week thinking about these things, what was the most important thing you learned? How did God speak to you this week?

2. Who is your favorite character in the Bible, and what character would you like to study in the Bible?

3. Describe how to do a character study—what tools would you use, and how can it be accomplished? How does looking at someone's life help you in your own life?

4. We also looked at doctrine and ethics study. How will knowing what we believe help us in our lives?

DAY 20: Those Who Have Gone Before Us

1. Who is your favorite hero of the Christian faith?

2. What Christian book has impacted your life the most?

3. What Bible study tool are you interested in learning about and incorporating into your quiet time? (As a leader, make certain your group knows about the Bible study tools in appendix 4.)

DAY 21: Communion with Jesus

1. Why is Jesus the best friend you'll ever have?

2. What was the most important truth you learned about Jesus?

3. How have you experienced the Lord Jesus in your own life?

DAY 22: When You See the Face of God

1. Day 22 begins with this statement: "The face of God shines from every page of the Bible." How have you come to know God more in the Bible?

2. What did you learn about yourself as you thought through the spiritual inventory questions? In what ways can a spiritual inventory be invaluable in your relationship with the Lord?

3. What does it mean to form a resolve or conviction from what you have learned in the Bible? Have you formed a resolve or conviction that has made a difference in your own life?

DAY 23: Praying the Bible

1. How does God's Word change the way you think?

2. You read about the kinds of discoveries you will make about God. Which discovery have you made, and how has that discovery made a difference in your life?

3. What did you think about the idea of praying verses and passages of Scripture in the Bible? Have you ever done that, and if so, what happened?

DAY 24: Experiencing the Romance Quiet Time

1. What did you learn from the life of George Mueller?

2. What is the value of praying God's Word?

3. What was the most important truth you learned from your quiet time?

4. Was there a favorite verse, quote, or insight you would like to share?

WEEK FIVE—ENJOY THE ROMANCE

DAY 25: Life in the Word

1. What a journey we have enjoyed as we have explored knowing and loving the Bible and coming face-to-face with God. You have spent 30 days focusing on the magnificent beauty of the Bible that you hold in your hands. This is not really an ending but a beginning as you apply all that you have learned about devotional Bible study. Think about the ideas you would like to implement to enrich your quiet time.

2. As you have now finished reading *Knowing and Loving the Bible,* what is the most important truth or insight you've learned as a result of the journey? How will this book and its emphasis on the Bible make a difference in your life? How has it changed your view of the Bible?

3. In day 25 you had the opportunity to think about the eternal perspective. Describe what it means to have an eternal perspective.

4. Why is the Bible essential to gaining an eternal perspective in life?

5. Why is it imperative that we have an eternal perspective? How will it help you in life?

DAY 26: The Life of Prayer

1. In day 26 we thought about unceasing prayer. What does it mean to pray without ceasing?

2. How does the Word of God encourage this life of prayer?

DAY 27: Ministry: Jesus Christ in Action

1. In day 27, you read about ministry. How does ministry come from your time with God in His Word?

2. Has God ever given you an idea for a ministry? What did you do with that idea?

3. How has the Bible encouraged you in your present ministry?

DAY 28: How to Start a Revival

1. Day 28 begins this way: "Jesus wants to start a revival in you and through you." How does the Word of God revive you?

2. Why is the church in need of revival?

3. How can we make a difference in our homes, community, churches, nation, and world?

DAY 29: The Ripple Effect

1. In day 29 you looked at the ripple effect. Describe what the ripple effect is and what it looks like in real life.

2. What kinds of decisions do we need to make to be a part of God's ripple effect?

DAY 30: Enjoying the Romance Quiet Time

1. What did you learn about the value of the Word of God in helping you see eternal things?

2. In what way can you "touch the hem of His garment" when you open the Bible?

3. As you think about your journey over the last 30 days, what has been most significant to you?

4. What is the most important thing you have learned in this 30-day journey of knowing and loving the Bible? What will you take with you from this time?

5. Who was your favorite example? What was your favorite verse or favorite quote?

6. Would you like to share anything else as a result of your 30-day journey?

7. Close in prayer.

MAKE A MEMORIAL
TO THE LORD

Then the LORD said to Moses, 'Write
this in a book as a memorial and recite
it to Joshua...' Moses built an altar and
named it The LORD is My Banner.

EXODUS 17:14-16

These stones shall become a memorial
to the sons of Israel forever.

JOSHUA 4:7

Throughout the Old Testament, the Lord often directed His people to write and remember, to set up visual reminders of His awesome acts, and to make memorials to Him all along the journey of life. Today, as a memorial to the Lord, take some time to reflect on your relationship with God over this last year.

1. What people have been most significant in your relationship with the Lord this year, and why?

2. What events have been significant to your relationship with the Lord and your spiritual growth this last year, and why?

3. What books has God used in your life this last year, and why were they important to you?

4. Did you have a word and verse this last year? If so, what were they?

5. What are the most important principles you have learned from the Lord in this last year?

6. What has God revealed to you about Himself this last year that has been most important to you?

7. Ask God to give you a new word and verse for this new year. If you know what they are, write them out.

8. Paul encourages us with the following words: "Do you not know that those who run in a race all run, but only one receives the prize? Run in such a way that you may win...I run in such a way, as not without aim" (1 Corinthians 9:24-27).

   Take some time now and ask God to give you goals for this new year. Write them out in the space below. Make them tangible goals and include the books you'd like to read this year, things you'd like to do, ministry objectives, and where you'd like to study in His Word either topically or by book of the Bible.

9. As you close this time of making a memorial to the Lord your God, read back through what you have written and all that God has done in your life. Then, draw near to Him in gratefulness and praise for who He is. You may even want to write out your prayer to Him, expressing what is on your heart.

Appendix 3

DEVOTIONAL
BIBLE STUDIES

For all these studies you will need your Bible and a journal or the Quiet Time Notebook additional Devotional Bible Study pages.

OBSERVATION STUDY

Recommended tools: cross-reference Bible

Study goal: to learn spiritual principles for your life related to a biblical word, topic, character, or event

1. Choose a word, topic, character, or event from your passage.

2. Write the subject of your study in your journal or Observation Study page (see figure 2 on page 143). Be sure to put today's date so you can keep a chronicle of your journey with the Lord. Then record what passage of Scripture you are studying.

3. As you observe each truth about a repeated word, topic, Bible character, or event, write out what you see, fact by

fact. If you have time, record the verses related to each observation.

4. Once you have recorded what you have seen, summarize what you have learned in two to three sentences.

5. Write in one sentence how you can apply what you have learned to your own life.

Suggested observation studies: the Lord in Psalm 139, Ezra in Ezra 7–10, suffering in Philippians, hope in 1 Peter, Jesus in Revelation 1:13-20

TRANSLATION STUDY

Recommended tools: NASB, NIV

Optional tools: AMP, NLT, MSG, Williams New Testament, ESV

Study goal: to understand the meaning of a verse by examining various Bible translations with life application

1. Record your verse in your journal or on a Translation Study page (see figure 3 on page 144).

2. Choose at least two translations and write out the verse from each translation word for word. If you have access to the Internet, use the many Bible translations available online at www.biblegateway.com. Without the Internet, use the *Comparative Study Bible,* which offers four translations (KJV, AMP, NASB, NIV), or Bible study software.

3. Moving from phrase to phrase, examine your verse in each translation and/or paraphrase, and note the differences among the versions. Record your observations.

4. Summarize how your observations provide insight into the meaning of the verse. Choose your favorite translation of the verse and write out why you like it so much.

5. Write in one sentence how you can apply what you have learned to your own life

Suggested translation studies: Jeremiah 29:11; John 14:26; Romans 12:1-2; Hebrew 1:3, 11:1.

VERSE STUDY

Recommended tools: exhaustive concordance, Hebrew-Greek *Key Word Study Bible, The Complete Wordstudy Old Testament* and *New Testament*

Optional tools: *The Complete Wordstudy Dictionary: New Testament, Theological Wordbook of the Old Testament, Vine's Expository Dictionary, Wuest's Word Studies in the Greek New Testament*

Study goal: to appreciate the beauty of biblical words in their original language, gaining deeper insight into the meaning with life application

1. Select a verse that impresses you, a significant verse from a passage you are reading and studying, and write the complete verse in your journal or on a Verse Study page (see figure 9 on page 153).

2. Choose at least two important words in your verse and write them in your journal (leaving space for *Strong's* number and definitions) or in the spaces provided on the Verse Study page.

3. Using your exhaustive concordance, *Key Word Study Bible,* or *Complete Wordstudy Old* or *New Testament,* record the *Strong's* number for each word in its corresponding space (see figures 4 and 5, page 149).

4. Using the *Key Word Study Bible, The Complete Wordstudy Old* or *New Testament,* or optional tools, define each word.

5. Review the context of your verse (cultural and biblical context including author and date) through your own observation and by consulting a study Bible, a Bible dictionary or encyclopedia, or a commentary.

6. Review your word definitions and summarize your conclusions on the meaning of your verse.

7. Write in one sentence how you can apply what you have learned to your own life.

Suggested verse studies: Psalm 27:14; Jeremiah 29:11; 31:3; John 1:14; 3:16; Ephesians 1:7,18; 3:17; 6:12; Hebrews 1:3; 11:1; James 1:3;4:8

WORD STUDY

Recommended tools: exhaustive concordance, Hebrew-Greek *Key Word Study Bible, The Complete Wordstudy Old* and *New Testament,* Hebrew concordance coded to *Strong's*

Optional tools: *The Complete Wordstudy Dictionary: New Testament, Theological Wordbook of the Old Testament, Vine's Expository Dictionary, Wuest's Word Studies in the Greek New Testament, Linguistic Key to the Greek New Testament*

Study goal: to gain a more complete picture of the meaning of a word in the original Greek or Hebrew with life application

1. Select a word that impresses you, a significant word from a passage you are reading and studying, and record the word in your journal or on a Word Study page (see figure 10 on page 154).

2. Using your exhaustive concordance, *Key Word Study Bible,* or *The Complete Wordstudy Old* or *New Testament,* record the *Strong's* number for your word.

3. Record the Scripture passage that contains the word.

4. Record the Hebrew or Greek transliteration of your word (the English phonetic equivalent for the Hebrew or Greek word. You can find this in the lexical aids in the *Key Word Study Bible* or the *Strong's* dictionary).

5. Record any other ways this Hebrew or Greek word has been translated into English by looking in other English translations of the Bible.

6. Look in the *Strong's Exhaustive Concordance* dictionary and write out the brief definition in your notebook or on the Word Study page.

7. Look up the word in *Vine's Expository Dictionary* (if available) and record its definition.

8. Record definitions from either the *Key Word Study Bible,* The *Complete Wordstudy New* or *Old Testament* lexical aids,

The Complete Wordstudy Dictionary: New Testament, or *Theological Wordbook of the Old Testament* (if available).

9. Choose any additional word study tools (if available) and record the definitions. Make certain that additional word study tools are keyed to the *Strong's* numbers if you do not know the original Hebrew and Greek languages. Some word study tools such as *Wuest's Word Studies in the Greek New Testament* are written in verse order for certain books of the Bible. These types of tools are especially easy to use since you only need to look up the chapter and verse and then read all that the author has to say about the words in that verse

10. Using the Greek concordance found in back of *The Complete Wordstudy New Testament,* or a Hebrew or Greek concordance keyed to the *Strong's* numbers such as *Wigram's Englishman's Hebrew Concordance* or *Greek Concordance,* look up your Hebrew or Greek word using the *Strong's* number. Record all the verses using your word from the book of the Bible containing the word you are studying. As you look up each verse and record your insights, you will be learning how the author has used this same Hebrew or Greek word in other parts of the book God has inspired him to write.

11. Record other verses found in the Old or New Testament that contain your Hebrew or Greek word. As you look up each verse and record your insights, you will be learning how other authors have used this same Hebrew or Greek word.

12. Review all your definitions and summarize what you believe this word means.

13. To keep your word definition in context, write in one sentence why the author chose this word and how it helps you understand the selected verse or passage of study.

14. Write in one sentence how you can apply what you have learned to your own life.

Suggested word studies: *faith* in Hebrews 11:1, *perseverance* in James 1:12, *blessed* in Matthew 5:3, *love* in 1 Corinthians 13:1, *prayed* in James 5:17, *humbled* in Philippians 2:8

Reference Study

Recommended tools: cross-reference Bible

Optional tools: The *New Treasury of Scripture Knowledge*

Study goal: to discover the whole counsel of God's Word about the meaning of a particular phrase in the Bible with life application

1. Select a favorite phrase from the Bible.

2. Find the letter of the alphabet at the beginning of the selected phrase in your cross-reference Bible (see figure 6 on page 151).

3. Find the verse number in the margin and the letter of the alphabet following that number. Next to the letter will be one or more cross-references.

4. Write down each reference in your journal or on a Reference Study page.

5. Look up each reference in your Bible and write out your insights.

6. Summarize what you have learned from your study.

7. Write in one sentence how you can apply what you have learned to your own life.

Suggested reference studies: Psalm 46:1; 84:11; 91:1; John 1:1; 16:33; Ephesians 1:3; Philippians 4:6-7

Topical Study

Recommended tools: cross-reference Bible, concordance

Optional tools: *Nave's Topical Bible*

Study goal: to discover the whole counsel of God's Word about a topic in the Bible with life application

1. Select a favorite word or topic from the Bible.

2. Look in *Nave's Topical Bible* or a concordance and find that word.

3. Write down as many of the references as desired in your journal or on a Reference (Topical) Study page.

4. Look up each verse in your Bible and write out your insights.

5. Summarize what you have learned from your study.

6. Write in one sentence how you can apply what you have learned to your own life.

Suggested topical studies: hope, trust, joy, Jesus, love, peace, marriage, children, suffering, holiness

CHARACTER STUDY

Recommended tools: cross-reference Bible, exhaustive concordance

Optional tools: *Nave's Topical Bible, Thompson Chain Reference Bible, International Standard Bible Encyclopedia, New Bible Dictionary*

Study goal: Your goal in this study is to form spiritual principles from a Bible character's life that will help you walk more closely with the Lord. Sometimes your key passages will be your immediate area of study. Other times your immediate area of study simply mentions the person's name, and you need to search out the main passages using a concordance, topical Bible, or Bible dictionary or encyclopedia. This can be accomplished by cross-referencing the verse in the immediate area of study, by looking up the person's name in your exhaustive concordance, and by looking up the person's name in *Nave's Topical Bible* or in the back of *Thompson Chain Reference Bible.*

1. Record the character you have chosen and the area of study that prompted you to choose this person in your journal or on a Character Study page.

2. Once you find the person's name, write down the most frequently referenced passages in your journal or on a Character Study page.

3. You may choose to look at each passage, recording your observations. However, it is most beneficial to choose only one or two main passages to study in one sitting. This allows

you to spend more time making observations. Turn to a number of the passages, asking God to guide you in your choice of passages.

4. Read your chosen passages slowly, verse by verse, recording as you read

    a. what you notice about this person's life

    b. insights related to their character

    c. the important events in their life

    d. the quality of their relationship with God.

Write your observations.

5. After you have read verse by verse, recording your observations, think about what you have observed. Summarize your significant observations of their life, major character qualities, important life events, and relationship with God. Write a summary.

6. Using the *International Standard Bible Encyclopedia,* the *New Bible Dictionary,* or other encyclopedias, dictionaries, and biographies, record any additional insights.

7. Summarize significant principles learned from the person's life.

8. Write in one sentence how you can apply what you have learned to your own life.

Suggested Character Studies: *Abraham* in Genesis 12–15; 22; *Joseph* in Genesis 37–45; *Moses* in Exodus 3; *Joshua* in Joshua 1–8; 23–24; *Deborah* in Judges 4–5; *Ruth* in Ruth 1–4; *David* in 1 Samuel 16–17; *David* in 2 Samuel 5–9; 11–12; 22–24; *Mary* in Luke 1–2; *Elizabeth* and *Zacharias* in Luke 1; *Saul/Paul* in Acts 7:57–9:31; and *John* in Revelation 1; 22.

DOCTRINE OR ETHICS STUDY

Recommended tools: cross-reference Bible, Quiet Time Notebook, exhaustive concordance

Optional tools: *Nave's Topical Bible, Thompson Chain Reference Bible, The Moody Handbook of Theology, Encyclopedia of Biblical and Christian Ethics, International Standard Bible Encyclopedia, New Bible Dictionary*

Study goal: to know what you believe and apply it to your life

1. Select a doctrine or ethic and write the topic in your journal or on a Doctrine or Ethics page.

2. Record relevant Scriptures you have found in your daily Bible reading, your exhaustive concordance, *Nave's Topical Bible,* or *Thompson Chain Reference Bible.*

3. Next to each verse, write in one sentence how it sheds light on your selected doctrine or ethic.

4. Define any important words that are relevant to the doctrine or ethic.

5. Search other reference works, such as *The Moody Handbook of Theology, Encyclopedia of Biblical and Christian Ethics, International Standard Bible Encyclopedia,* and the *New Bible Dictionary* to learn more about your doctrine or ethic and to find any additional related verses.

6. Summarize your beliefs based on your findings.

7. Write in one sentence how you can apply what you have learned to your own life.

Suggested doctrine studies: the attributes and names of God, the attributes and names of Jesus Christ, the humanity and divinity of Christ, the Holy Spirit, the Trinity, man, sin, salvation, eternal security, the church, angels, future things (judgment, heaven, hell, the return of Christ, death, eternity). For additional specific doctrines, consult *The Moody Handbook of Theology.*

Suggested ethic studies: abortion, affluence, alcohol and social drinking, cheating, church and state, employment and work, family, fidelity and morality, homosexuality, leisure, lying and truthfulness, marriage, war, women in ministry, observing the Sabbath. For additional specific ethical issues consult *Encyclopedia of Biblical and Christian Ethics.*

BIBLE STUDY TOOLS

*You will find a more comprehensive
list at the Quiet Time Ministries
website at www.quiettime.org.*

The Carta Bible Atlas (formerly titled *The Macmillan Bible Atlas*) by Yohanan Aharoni (Jerusalem: Carta, 2003). One of the very best atlases of the Bible lands.

The Complete Wordstudy New Testament and *The Complete Wordstudy Old Testament,* edited by Spiros Zodhiates (Chattanooga: AMG Publishers, 1991, 1994). More comprehensive than the *Key Word Study Bible,* these tools assign *Strong's* numbers to every word in the Bible and include the same dictionaries as the *Key Word Study Bible* and a Hebrew/Greek concordance.

The Complete Wordstudy Dictionary: New Testament by Spiros Zodhiates, (Chattanooga: AMG Publishers, 1992). Definitions for every word in the Greek New Testament.

The Expositor's Bible Commentary, volumes 1–12, edited by Frank E. Gaebelein (Grand Rapids: Zondervan Publishing House, 1981). An excellent commentary set with reliable scholarship. May be purchased one volume at a time.

Halley's Bible Handbook by Henry H. Halley (Grand Rapids: Zondervan Publishing House, 1965). A concise handbook offering important information to help understand context.

The International Standard Biblical Encyclopedia, volumes 1–4, edited by Geoffrey W. Bromiley (Grand Rapids: William B. Eerdmans Publishing Co., 1986). Includes articles on people, places, and events in the Bible.

Key Word Study Bible (NASB) edited by Spiros Zodhiates (Chattanooga: AMG Publishers, 1990). Contains two Greek/Hebrew dictionaries with comprehensive and insightful definitions for most of the important words in the Bible. Also parses most of the important Greek verbs and includes grammatical explanations. Make certain that you get the NASB version of this Bible.

Linguistic Key to the Greek New Testament by Fritz Reinecker and Cleon Rogers (Grand Rapids: Zondervan Publishing House, 1976). Organized in the order of the New Testament, this reference defines all the most important words of the text (actual Greek words with English definitions) and parses all the major Greek verbs, using more than 300 sources.

Logos Bible study software. This is my favorite Bible software and adds to your library of study tools. I use this software to research and study for writing messages, articles, and books.

Matthew Henry's Commentary (Peabody, MA: Hendrickson Publishers, 1991). A wonderful devotional commentary on the whole Bible.

The Moody Handbook of Theology by Paul Enns (Chicago: Moody Press, 1989). Presents different views of all major doctrines in a fair and concise manner.

Nave's Topical Bible by Orville J. Nave (Peabody, MA: Hendrickson Publishers). This marvelous scholar spent a lifetime organizing Scripture references according to topic, and we can benefit from his labor.

New American Standard Exhaustive Concordance of the Bible, edited by Robert L. Thomas (Nashville: Holman Bible Publishers, 1981). Contains every occurrence of each word in the Bible. Uses *Strong's* numbering system for words.

New Bible Commentary, edited by D.A. Carson, R.T. France, J.A. Motyer, G.J. Wenham (Downers Grove: InterVarsity Press, 1994). An excellent scholarly one-volume commentary with insights for every passage in the Bible.

New Bible Dictionary, edited by J.D. Douglas (Grand Rapids: Zondervan Publishing House, 1999). Includes important information about people, places, events, and books of the Bible.

Theological Wordbook of the Old Testament by R. Laird Harris, Gleason L. Archer, and Bruce K. Waltke (Chicago: Moody Press, 1980). An invaluable two-volume study tool for understanding meanings of Old Testament words. Coded to *Strong's* numbering system.

The New Treasury of Scripture Knowledge, edited by Jerome H. Smith (Nashville: Thomas Nelson Publishers, 1992). An exciting cross-reference study tool. Arranged from Genesis to Revelation, cross-references are listed verse by verse and keyed to each important phrase.

Vine's Expository Dictionary of New Testament Words by W.E. Vine (Nashville: Thomas Nelson Publishers, 1985). Includes insightful definitions of key words in the Bible. Obtain the edition coded to the *Strong's* numbering system.

Wuest's Word Studies in the Greek New Testament by Kenneth Wuest (Grand Rapids: William B. Eerdmans Publishing Company, 1950). An excellent four-volume word study tool. Organized according to books in the New Testament, Wuest defines words verse by verse in many of the New Testament books. One of my favorites.

Zondervan NIV Atlas of the Bible by Carl G. Rasmussen (Grand Rapids: Zondervan Publishing House, 1989). Very helpful for understanding locations of places mentioned in Scripture.

Zondervan NIV Bible Commentary, edited by Kenneth L. Barker and John R. Kohlenberger (Grand Rapids: Zondervan Publishing House, 1994). An excellent two-volume commentary covering the entire Bible. These two volumes are a distillation of the twelve-volume *Expositor's Bible Commentary,* edited by Frank E. Gaebelein.

Zondervan NIV Exhaustive Concordance by Edward W. Goodrick and John R. Kohlenberger (Grand Rapids: Zondervan Publishers). Contains every occurrence of each word in the NIV translation of the Bible. Uses Strong's numbering system for words.

Zondervan Pictorial Encyclopedia of the Bible, edited by Merrill Tenney and Steven Barabas (Grand Rapids: Zondervan Publishing House, 1975). These five volumes are immensely helpful in understanding the people, events, background, and land of the Bible.

Appendix 5

PRAYERS IN
THE BIBLE

Prayer of Abraham—Genesis 18:16-33

Prayers by Moses—Exodus 33:12-18; Deuteronomy 32:1-4; Psalm 90

Prayer of Joshua—Joshua 7:6-9

Prayers in Judges—Judges 5

Prayers in Kings and Chronicles—1 Kings 13:6; 2 Kings 13:4; 22:18-19; 1 Chronicles 4:10; 16:7-36 (cf. Psalm 105); 29:10-20; 2 Chronicles 14:11; 15:3-4; 20:3-12; 33:10-13.

Hezekiah's prayer—2 Kings 19:15-19

Solomon's prayers—1 Kings 3:5-9; 1 Kings 8:22-62; 2 Chronicles 6:12-42

David's prayers—Psalms 3–9, 11–32, 34–42, 51–70, 86, 101, 103, 108–110, 122, 124, 138–145

Other prayers in the Psalms—see especially Psalm 91; 119

Jesus' prayers (The Lord's Prayer)—Matthew 6:9-13; Luke 11:2-4

Paul's prayers—Romans 1:8-10; 1 Corinthians 1:4-9; Ephesians 1:15-19; 3:14-21; Philippians 1:3-10; Colossians 1:9-12; 1 Thessalonians 1:2-3; 2 Thessalonians 1:3

NOTES

Epigraph

From *Annie Johnson Flint's Best-Loved Poems* (Toronto: Evangelical Publishers), pp.42-43.

Day 1—The Invitation to the Divine Romance

1. A.W. Tozer, *The Pursuit of God* (Camp Hill, PA: Christian Publications 1982, 1993), p. 70.

Day 3—Why I Love the Bible

1. *Studies in the Sermon on the Mount* by Oswald Chambers, 1995 by Oswald Chambers Publishing Association, Ltd. and is used by permission of Discovery House Publishers, Grand Rapids, MI 49501. All rights reserved.

2. Taken from Linguistic Key to the Greek New Testament, One-Volume by CLEON L. ROGERS JR.; FRITZ RIENECKER. Copyright © by The Zondervan Corporation. Used by permission of The Zondervan Corporation. Page 581.

3. Edwin Hodder, "Thy Word Is like a Garden, Lord," *The New Sunday School Hymn Book,* 1863.

DAY 4—THE SECRET GARDEN OF GOD'S WORD

1. Frances Hodgson Burnett, *The Secret Garden* (New York: HarperCollins Publishers).

2. Marvin Wilson, *Our Father Abraham* (Grand Rapids: William B. Eerdmans Publishing Company, 1989), pp. 287-88.

DAY 5—THE TREASURE OF GOD'S WORD

1. Howard Hendricks, *Living by the Book* (Chicago: Moody Press, 1991), p. 19.

2. Taken from The Challenge of Bible Translation by GLEN G. SCORGIE; MARK L. STRAUSS; STEVEN M. VOTH. Copyright © 2003 by Glen G. Scorgie, Mark L. Strauss, and Steven M. Voth. Used by permission of The Zondervan Corporation. pp. 20-21.

3. J. Robertson McQuilken, *Understanding and Applying the Bible* (Chicago: Moody Press, 1983), page 69.

4. See Josh McDowell, *Guide to Understanding Your Bible* (San Bernardino, CA: Here's Life Publishers, 1982), p. 6.

5. Paul Enns, *The Moody Handbook of Theology* (Chicago: Moody Press, 1989), p. 160.

6. Ibid., p. 170.

7. Available online at www.iclnet.org/pub/resources/text/history/chicago.stm.txt.

8. Taken from From Ancient Tab 2 Mod Trans by DAVID EWERT. Copyright © 1983 by The Zondervan Corporation. Used by permission of The Zondervan Corporation. Pages 19-20.

9. Ibid., p. 186.

10. G.W. Bromiley. *The International Standard Bible Encyclopedia,* vol. 2 (Grand Rapids: Wm. B. Eerdmans, 2001), p. 114.

11. Ewert, p. 189.

Day 8—The Truth About Truth

1. Alan Bloom, *The Closing of the American Mind* (New York: Simon & Schuster Inc., 1987), p. 25.

2. Ravi Zacharias, "The Inextinguishable Light." Available online at www .rzim.org/publications/jttran.php?seqid=38.

3. Spiros Zodhiates, *The Complete Word Study Dictionary,* (Chattanooga, TN: AMG Publishers, 1992), p. 120.

4. Charles Colson and Nancy Pearcey, *How Now Shall We Live* (Wheaton, IL: Tyndale House Publishers, Inc., 1999), p. 37.

Day 9—It Really Is True!

1. Howard F. Vox, *Archaeology in Bible Lands* (Chicago: Moody Press, 1977), p. 16.

2. Keith N. Schoville, *Biblical Archaeology in Focus* (Grand Rapids: Baker Book House, 1978), pp. 242-246. Used by permission.

3. Details of this discovery may be found at www.mcmaster.ca/ua/opr/nms/ newsreleases/2004adams.html.

4. Schoville, p. 447.

Day 10—The Holy Spirit and the Word

1. James Montgomery Boice, "Reformed Theology." Available online at www .graceonlinelibrary.org/articles/full.asp?id-13|47|596.

2. J. Hampton Keathley, "The Bible: Understanding Its Message." Available online at www.bible.org/page.asp?page_id-698.

3. Charles Ryrie, *The Ryrie Study Bible* (Chicago: Moody Press), p. 618.

Day 11—The Ground of Your Heart

1. William Shannon, *Seeking the Face of God* (New York: Crossroad Publishing Company, 1988), p. 42.

2. Taken from Linguistic Key to the Greek New Testament, One-Volume by CLEON L. ROGERS JR.; FRITZ RIENECKER. Copyright © by The Zondervan Corporation. Used by permission of The Zondervan Corporation. Page 523.

DAY 14—DISCOVERING SECRETS IN THE WORD

1. Merrill C. Tenney, *Galatians: The Charter of Christian Liberty* (Grand Rapids: Wm. B. Eerdmans Publishing Company, 1960), pp. 207-08.

DAY 15—ENGAGING IN THE ROMANCE

1. J.I. Packer, *Knowing God* (Downers Grove, IL: InterVarsity Press, 1975), pp. 18-19.

2. See How to Read the Bible for All Its Worth by DOUGLAS K. STUART; GORDON D. FEE. Copyright © 1981, 1993, 2003 by Douglas Stuart and Gordon D. Fee. Used by permission of The Zondervan Corporation. page. 21.

DAY 18—QUIET TIME WEEK THREE: EXPLORING THE ROMANCE

1. Amy Carmichael, "A Joy to Thee," in *Mountain Breezes* (Fort Washington, PA: Christian Literature Crusade, 1999), p. 182. Used by permission.

2. G. Campbell Morgan, *The Westminster Pulpit* (Grand Rapids: Baker Book House, 2006), vol. 8, p. 178.

3. Ibid., vol. 2, pp. 278-80.

4. Ibid., vol. 5, pp. 62-64.

DAY 19—TRANSFORMED BY THE BIBLE

1. Quoted in Richard Ellsworth Day, *The Shadow of the Broad Brim*, (Philadelphia: The Judson Press, 1934), p. 138.

DAY 20—THOSE WHO HAVE GONE BEFORE US

1. Quoted in Richard Ellsworth Day, *The Shadow of the Broad Brim*, p. 122.

2. You can take an online tour of Spurgeon's library housed at William Jewell College at www.spurgeon.org/fsl.htm.

DAY 23—PRAYING THE BIBLE

1. From M.R. DeHaan, *Broken Things* (Grand Rapids: Discovery House Publishers, 1989).

DAY 24—QUIET TIME WEEK FOUR: EXPERIENCING THE ROMANCE

1. A.T. Pierson, *George Mueller of Bristol,* (New York: Fleming H. Revell), pp. 140-141.

2. Ibid., pp. 93-97.

DAY 25—LIFE IN THE WORD

1. Elisabeth Elliot, *The Shadow of the Almighty* (San Francisco Harper-SanFrancisco, 1989).

DAY 28—HOW TO START A REVIVAL

1. See George Barna's book, *If Things Are So Good, Then Why Do I Feel So Bad?* (Chicago, IL: Moody Press, 1994), p. 245.

ACKNOWLEDGMENTS

Thank you to my family—David, Mother, Dad, Rob, Tania, Christopher, Kayla, Eloise, Ann, Andy, Keegan, and James—for your constant love and encouragement. I especially thank my husband, David, who has tirelessly helped with the editing of my books, the design of all our websites, and the development of our quiet time resources.

Thank you to Kayla, my assistant in Quiet Time Ministries, who helps me in every aspect of ministry from writing books and speaking to developing and producing resources for others to grow in their quiet times. Thank you to Shelley, my assistant at Southwest Community Church, who helps me in everything involved with serving our women. Thank you to our Quiet Time Ministries team for your prayers and involvement: Conni Hudson, Shirley Peters, Cindy Clark, Kelly Abeyratne, and Paula Zillmer. Thank you to those who piloted *Knowing and Loving the Bible*— Nancy Brown, Ceil Burns, Cheryle Clark, Donna Delahanty, Craig and Meachele Campbell, Diani Rodica-Virginia, Kelly Abeyratne, Kayla Branscum, Jane Harris, Joan Hill, Patty Hill, Leah Hudson, Dawn Ivie, Carolyn Joy, Davida Kreisler, Debi Linker, Shirley Peters, Kate Storset, Sherlen Yoak, Paula Zillmer, Julie Airis, Cay Hough, Betty Mann, Myra Murphy, Kathleen Otremba, Sandi Rogers, and Sharon Hasting. As always, Conni Hudson, thank you for your incredible leadership of our pilots for everything I write. Thank you to the *Enriching Your Quiet Time* magazine staff for helping develop the ideas for the books I write: Shirley Peters, Maurine Cromwell, Cay Hough, Conni Hudson. Thank you to those who partner financially with us in Quiet Time Ministries, enabling us to carry out so many exciting opportunities entrusted to us by the Lord. Thank you to our Quiet Time Ministries board of directors for your wise counsel and teamwork.

Thank you to the women at Southwest Community Church, who are an absolute joy to me as we serve the Lord together. Thank you to the pastors and church staff for your love and leadership.

Thank you to special friends who have given me a listening ear and a timely word when I needed it: Beverly Trupp, Andy Kotner, Julie Airis, Helen Peck, Betty and Johnny Mann, Myra Murphy, my Quiet Time Ministry team, Sandi Rogers, and Kathleen Otremba.

Thank you to those who have been examples to me in knowing and loving the Bible: Josh and Dottie McDowell, Bill and Vonette Bright,

Kay Arthur, Elmer Lappen, Leann Pruitt McGee, Dr. Ron Youngblood, Dr. Walt Wessel, and Dr. Al Glenn.

A special thank you to Jim Smoke, who has been used by the Lord to open so many doors for my ministry. Thank you to Greg Johnson of WordServe Literary Group for encouraging me to write the books on my heart. Thank you to Mark Lundeen, research assistant to Josh McDowell, for his help with archaeological discoveries related to the Bible.

Thank you to Harvest House Publishers for your vision and godly leadership. A special thanks to Bob Hawkins Sr. for your contribution to Christian publishing. Thank you to Bob Hawkins Jr. for your leadership and for encouraging me in Quiet Time Ministries. Thank you to Gene Skinner for all your help in the editing of this book. Thank you to Terry Glaspey for your encouragement as I write the books that the Lord gives me to write. And thank you to the entire Harvest House team in working together with me to get this book to those who desire to know and love the Bible.

Finally, thank you to those who lead others to know and love the Bible throughout the world: pastors, women's ministries directors, ministry leaders, Bible study leaders, and bookstore owners and staff. May you continue to let your light shine that others may catch the excitement and open the pages of their Bible and hear God speak.

ABOUT THE AUTHOR

Catherine Martin is a summa cum laude graduate of Bethel Theological Seminary with a Master of Arts Degree in Theological Studies. She is founder and president of Quiet Time Ministries, director of women's ministries at Southwest Community Church in Indian Wells, California, and adjunct faculty member of Biola University. She is author of *Six Secrets to a Powerful Quiet Time* and *Knowing and Loving the Bible,* published by Harvest House Publishers, and *Pilgrimage of the Heart, Revive My Heart!* and *A Heart That Dances,* published by NavPress. She has also written the *Quiet Time Notebook, A Heart On Fire, A Heart to See Forever,* and *The Quiet Time Classic Collection,* published by Quiet Time Ministries Press. She is also senior editor for *Enriching Your Quiet Time* quarterly magazine. As a popular speaker at retreats and conferences, Catherine challenges others to seek God and love Him with all of one's heart, soul, mind, and strength.

About Quiet Time Ministries

Quiet Time Ministries is a nonprofit corporation that offers books, magazines, and videos for your quiet time. Visit Quiet Time Ministries online at www.quiettime.org. The Quiet Time Ministries Resources and Training Center located in Bermuda Dunes, California, offers conferences and workshops to encourage others in their relationship with the Lord.

Quiet Time Ministries
Post Office Box 14007
Palm Desert, CA 92255
1-800-925-6458
760-772-2357
www.quiettime.org

OTHER *KNOWING AND LOVING THE BIBLE* RESOURCES
available from Quiet Time Ministries

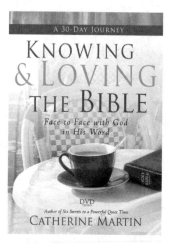

Companion DVD

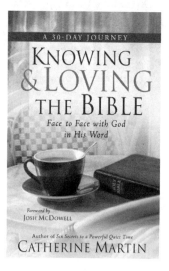

Companion Journal